S0-BRW-631

SIDESTEP
&
TWIST

SIDESTEP
&
TWIST

JAMES GARDNER

Marshall Cavendish
Business

Copyright © 2012 James Gardner
Cover design: OpalWorks Pte Ltd

Published in 2011 by Marshall Cavendish Business
An imprint of Marshall Cavendish International

PO Box 65829, London EC1P 1NY, United Kingdom
info@marshallcavendish.co.uk

and

1 New Industrial Road, Singapore 536196
genrefsales@sg.marshallcavendish.com
www.marshallcavendish.com/genref

Other Marshall Cavendish offices: Marshall Cavendish Corporation. 99 White
Plains Road, Tarrytown NY 10591-9001, USA • Marshall Cavendish International
(Thailand) Co Ltd. 253 Asoke, 12th Flr, Sukhumvit 21 Road, Klongtoey Nua,
Wattana, Bangkok 10110, Thailand • Marshall Cavendish (Malaysia) Sdn Bhd. Times
Subang, Lot 46, Subang Hi-Tech Industrial Park, Batu Tiga, 40000 Shah Alam,
Selangor Darul Ehsan, Malaysia

Marshall Cavendish is a trademark of Times Publishing Limited

The right of James Gardner to be identified as the authors of this work has been
asserted by them in accordance with the Copyright, Designs and Patents Act 1988.

All rights reserved

No part of this publication may be reproduced, stored in a retrieval system or
transmitted, in any form or by any means, electronic, mechanical, photocopying,
recording or otherwise, without the prior permission of the copyright owner. Requests
for permission should be addressed to the publisher. The author and publisher have
used their best efforts in preparing this book and disclaim liability arising directly
and indirectly from the use and application of this book. All reasonable efforts have
been made to obtain necessary copyright permissions. Any omissions or errors are
unintentional and will, if brought to the attention of the publisher, be corrected in
future printings.

A CIP record for this book is available from the British Library

ISBN 978-981-4351-10-2

Printed and bound in Great Britain by
TJ International Ltd, Padstow, Cornwall

mc Marshall Cavendish publishes an exciting range of books
on business, management and self-development.

If you would like to:
• Find out more about our titles
• Take advantage of our special offers
• Sign up to our e-newsletter

Please visit our
special website at: www.business-bookshop.co.uk

To my Grandmothers, who passed on during the writing.
And my Grandfather, who remains with us still.

CONTENTS

PREFACE

This is a book I've been thinking about for some time. At the height of the dot-com boom, in 2000, I was working in a software start-up that built internet banking software. We did well enough to put food on the table, but we weren't earning the kind of money you'd expect from an industry at the peak of a veritable wave of hype.

The thing was, lots of other people were *also* making internet banking software. The field became increasingly crowded as everyone with any remotely aligned technology poured into the market. It didn't matter how good *our* product was, as there simply wasn't enough business to go around.

As soon as the bubble burst and funding ran out, the company closed. I would not work in a small company again for more than a decade, choosing the relative safety of large software firms like Microsoft, banks and government institutions.

But the experience left me asking a question: why, when we were first to the market with an innovative product, did we not dominate by default? What did we do wrong that let us squander our first-mover advantage? It was a question that bothered me for years, not in the least because (later, as a technology buyer) I saw companies with astounding innovations, first-of-a-kind technologies that *should* have won, fail time after time in the face of copy-cat competitors.

At the time, I was fully convinced the difference between corporate greatness and mediocrity was the quality and uniqueness of ideas. I believed great companies were made when you had the best quality talent, particularly those with the most original thinking.

But if that were true, I wondered, how come the great ideas coming across my desk weren't making much money for their owners? I began to lose faith in the power of creativity as a driver of new value. I resigned myself to a world in which creativity was for artists, not business people. Execution, I concluded, was the driving difference between success and failure. The talented people companies needed, obviously, were those who were great at making things happen.

I was correct in one thing: ideas *aren't* all that valuable a commodity. But I was wrong in thinking that *only* great execution separated amazing companies from merely adequate ones. I began to study hit companies with hit products, wondering what this execution secret sauce might be. And slowly, so slowly, I came to realise that some of the fundamental things I'd always believed about the process of innovation in corporations was wrong.

You don't need to have the best talent to win. You don't need to be superlative at execution to succeed. These are both capabilities that are *helpful*, but it may be they're much less important that we'd previously believed.

In this book, I'll try to explain why I've come to this conclusion. Together, we'll explore cases where genius didn't lead to particularly significant financial rewards, and others where slavishly following the pack created the Wealth of Nations. In these pages you'll find an explanation of how outcomes such as these can occur, despite the value corporations have traditionally placed on breakthroughs and innovation as a driver of value. I hope that by the end you'll have a different perspective on the process of creating new products and services in organisations, even if you do not agree with my fundamental premise.

It is necessary, at this point, for me to explain that this is a book that's the sum of the insights and observations of a great many people. It is therefore appropriate that I acknowledge their contributions before proceeding much farther.

Firstly, I want to thank all the people working in so many companies around the world who have given me access to their organisations and their time. Without fail, they've provided valuable criticism and advice, even when they didn't believe the basic premise of *Sidestep & Twist*. It is, after all, a premise that's somewhat challenging for anyone who's been involved in traditional research and development for any period of time. We all want to believe our creativity is the driving force in value creation, even though it seems it isn't most of the time.

There are other people who have made important contributions to this book, too. My partner, my friends, colleagues and family have had to put up with almost a year of constant complaining that "I can't come out, I have to write", resulting in me missing a string of birthdays, anniversaries and other important dates. To my Twitter followers, whom every day or so had to put up with me complaining about "writers block", a problem more accurately described as "writers' procrastination".

And most especially, I need to thank all those who have worked in various innovation teams I've led over the last decade or so. Every one of you has contributed to *Sidestep & Twist* in some way. Each success and every failure has taught me something I would not have learned without being at your side. Because innovation management is such a new discipline, I can't help but wonder how much progress we would have made had we not been together.

I also want to acknowledge my colleagues at Spigit, the innovation software company. They were the first to see the material in any substantial way, and have been supportive throughout the whole process of turning it into a book. They were supportive even at the end of each financial quarter, when we were all dashing around to make some very ambitious financials.

A special acknowledgement is due to Geoff Connolly in Australia, amongst the first to read the manuscript. His candid, no-holds-barred feedback caused me to rethink many of my arguments throughout.

Finally, the last words of this preface are to the memory of both my grandmothers, who passed away during the course of the writing. Neither got much chance to be part of my work, but they were so proud I was "writing another book". I travelled to both funerals in Australia from London, also attended by my grandfather, who is still with us. To him, and the memory of those passed, I hope this book is appropriately dedicated.

INTRODUCTION

CHAPTER ONE

One of the greatest myths of our time is this: if you create something original, something that's genuinely a breakthrough, you have a better than average chance of getting rich.

For most businesses and most entrepreneurs, this notion is something of a fantasy. If you think back over the great corporate successes of the last two or so decades, you'll find a striking absence of any great breakthroughs significant enough in themselves to create huge wealth. On the other hand, many endeavours that *have* become hits are at best incremental improvements of other things.

It is a story I've found repeated time and time again, across sectors, countries, and cultures. Hit products and services are almost never genuinely original.

Some readers will be familiar with the top-selling drug of all time, a product called Lipitor, by Pfizer. It has broken all records in the deeply research-dependent drug business. But Lipitor wasn't all that new. It was the fifth drug in its class, and was just a bit stronger than what came before. Yet it has eclipsed all its competitors.

Even if you've never taken Lipitor, it is almost certain you've heard of the world's best selling book series. *Harry Potter*, by J.K. Rowling, is a publishing juggernaut. But *Harry Potter* is, in fact, based on a long tradition of stories set in British boarding schools, such as the famous *Tom Brown's School Days*, topped up with a smattering of slightly derivative fantasy. What many readers don't know, actually, is Britain's best-selling fantasy author prior to J.K. Rowling was Terry Pratchett, whose novel *Discworld* has a school for young magicians and a young wizard with dark hair and glasses.

A lack of genuine originality is a feature of almost every category-defining product in the last decade. Was Facebook the first social network? Certainly not: MySpace, Friendster and a host of others preceded it. In fact, the first real social network was a site called SixDegrees.com, and it was founded a decade before Facebook's meteoric rise began. Was it Google that created web search? Of course not: the company's contribution was to improve what Alta Vista and the other web search engines that had pioneered the field were doing already.

I could spend pages and pages going through examples like these, and will do so later on in this book. But one thing unites all these products and services: they're built on something that was working well somewhere else. There's another thing many of the great hits of the last decade have had in common: they've built their successes by creating value for customers that's independent of the features of the core product itself. Facebook, for example, is valuable not because it has the best and most features of any social network, but because most people are on Facebook. The more people who join Facebook, the better it functions for everyone.

Why is *Harry Potter* a money-printing machine for J.K. Rowling and her publishers? Of course the books are great sellers, but it is the ecosystem of complimentary products the franchise has spawned: movies, toys and games, homewares, posters, trivia and all the rest – which create the extraordinary demand for the novels among ever-widening audiences.

How did a few derivative fantasy books manage to create such an ecosystem of demand? Why is Facebook the premiere social network? The answer is simple. Both are products that get better the more they are used. This is true for many – perhaps all – category-defining products we've seen in recent years. And the key to all these successes is this: the sidestep and twist joins incrementally improving a product with a track record of working elsewhere with strategies that ensure it gets better as it is consumed.

At this point, a fundamental question raises its head. What happens to companies that *do* pursue creativity and genuine breakthroughs? In order to begin an answer to that question, let me tell you the story of a company that's been doing just this for a decade or more. We all know Microsoft, the most successful software company in the world. It is a company that achieved its dominance by means of clever business decisions it made in the early days of personal computing, decisions which resulted in the firm gaining near-monopoly positions in key product categories.

Microsoft today has some of the best business talent available, so it recognises it can't rely on these monopolies forever. For the last decade and more, therefore, it's been spending massively on research and development. In 2010 alone, the company spent more on R&D than any company has ever done in history. Despite investments of such magnitude, long-time rival Apple overtook Microsoft in market value in May 2010. By the middle of 2011, it had also exceeded Microsoft in both gross revenue and profit.

Apple's performance is surprising considering Microsoft has spent between two and three times as much on R&D as Apple every year. Over a couple of those years, in what must have been an absolute orgy of innovativeness, it spent almost 400% more. Microsoft's investments in looking for the next big breakthrough have been unprecedented, but none of this has made the slightest difference. It has failed to create very many new hits that can replace its rapidly eroding core businesses. Apple, on the other hand, has created hit after hit, and in the process has redefined key markets that used to be Microsoft mainstays.

Microsoft's recent history of underperformance – to which we'll return later – is counter intuitive, because we are conditioned to believe being first to do something is a recipe for success. For managers at the company, being first with new breakthroughs is a very rational investment that ought to have paid off.

Sadly, as we'll see in a moment, history is littered with the debris of genius that did things first. Great minds upon whose work our modern lives depend are very rarely the recipients of the market rewards their work has brought others. In fact, when you consider the top 10 scientific breakthroughs of the twentieth century, it is rare indeed to find a wealthy genius. On the other hand, it is nothing at all unusual to find stories where those who have taken the genius of others have gotten very rich indeed.

THE UN-WEALTHY GENIUS

To prove the point, let's turn to our first example: a man who changed the world by single-handedly creating the basis for modern electronics. Neither stupid nor lacking vision, this was a man who should have become one of the most wealthy individuals of all time. He should have been as wealthy as Microsoft's Bill Gates. Instead, Sir John Ambrose Fleming, inventor of the vacuum tube, lived to a ripe old age on his professorial pension, neither exceptionally wealthy nor particularly poor. His financial means remained modest, even as those who later used his invention as the basis for a whole new industry got incredibly rich.

Fleming was born in England in 1849, and lived most of his early years in London. He took a degree in physics, and this led to an interest in electricity and magnetism. It was the age of Thomas Edison (1847–1931), the American inventor who brought the world motion pictures and sound recordings. Surrounded by assistants, every conceivable machine tool, chemical stores and a comprehensive library, Edison was hard at work on what would become his greatest accomplishment: the electric light.

Electric lights were, apparently, hard to make. Though plenty of inventors before Edison had come up with lighting devices using electricity, every single one burnt out too quickly to be of any commercial use. In the end, Edison did crack the burn-out problem and proceeded to develop a whole electricity supply infrastructure necessary to enable the mass roll-out of his invention.

It was around this time that Fleming decided to supplement his income by working as a consultant with Edison's company. Some time after 1881, whilst on a visit to Edison's labs, he saw the great man demonstrate an interesting electrical effect. Edison, during his various light bulb experiments, had discovered an oddity: if you placed a filament in a vacuum and added a second electrode to which electricity could be applied, current would flow in one direction only. Fleming, when he saw the demonstration, did not immediately see much point in it. This would change a few years later.

Meanwhile, Fleming had moved on to working on transatlantic telegraphy. Though the first transatlantic telegraph cables had been laid in 1866 when Fleming was just 17 years old, the cost of using them was way out of reach of practically everyone. The cable had been laid at massive expense, some US$40 million (US$560 million in today's money). To get an understanding of how significant an investment this was, the doomed ship *Titanic*, the largest moving object ever built by man some 45 years later, cost a mere US$7 million dollars to construct.

Furthermore, the cable was inefficient compared to standard telegraphy. Able to send about 8 words a minute – a total of about 11,000 words a day – the limited capacity over such an expensive infrastructure increased the price per word ruinously. If you were to convert the charge into today's money, sending a word on these initial transatlantic cables would have cost somewhere between US$150 and US$200, depending on the exchange rate prevailing at the time.

Though instantaneous communication might have been out of reach of individuals, its advantages were self-evident for governments and industrialists, especially those with interests in far-flung corners of the globe. By the time Fleming was 27 years old, the British Empire had created a global telegraphic cable network that reached from London to all its dominions worldwide, including the remote colony in New Zealand. Though the cost was extraordinary, the machinery of government and commerce swiftly became addicted to the ability to send a few choice, meaning-laden words across the world.

It was demand for additional capacity that drove telegraphy companies to improve their methods quickly, but nothing came along to change the fact that cables were too expensive to make international communication routine. What was needed was wireless communication. Experimenters had shown it was possible to send messages without wires, but the technology didn't really exist to make it practical for any international distance. This challenge was one Fleming took up around his fiftieth birthday. That same year, 1899, he developed a crude device that worked experimentally.

The initial design may have worked as an experiment, but it was not a practical communications method by any means. Fleming was working with extraordinarily large voltages, way beyond those practical for any commercial application. Such voltages were needed because the available means for receiving transmissions were incredibly crude. The receiving device of choice was known as a coherer: a tube of iron filings with electrodes at each end. When such a tube is surrounded by a strong electromagnetic field, current is more easily able flow between the two electrodes. Measurement of this effect makes it possible to decode a message if the electric field is strong enough.

For Fleming and his device, creating an electric field powerful enough to span the ocean was the core of the problem. Electromagnetism is subject to an inverse square law. If, for example, you move a receiver three times as far away, you have to boost the power at the transmitter by nine times to have the same effect. You can imagine the hair-raisingly dangerous voltages Fleming was employing to get iron filings to move by a signal transmitted from the other side of the ocean.

But he had little choice but to work with the tools available if he wanted to make progress. Reasoning that boosting the power even more to improve capability simply wasn't the answer, he was forced to turn his attention to improvement of the coherer. Finally, all the pieces clicked together. What if he could use the obscure effect he'd seen Edison demonstrate to create a receiver that didn't use iron filings? Could it be possible the extra electrode in the Edison device could do the same job when connected to an appropriate antenna? In theory at least, such a device would be much more sensitive than the coherer, because radio waves wouldn't need to be strong enough to affect the physical iron atoms in the tube. Three years later, Fleming made it work. As he'd guessed, taking away the iron filings made a receiver that was incredibly sensitive. The power problem for wireless transmissions was solved.

Fleming wasn't stupid. He knew his invention had incredible implications, so he instantly filed a patent for the "Oscillation Valve", as he called it. Fleming's patent, when it was awarded shortly after, should have made him millions. It didn't.

What actually happened was another inventor, Lee De Forest (1873–1961), improved the oscillation valve by adding another wire attached to a grid inside the bulb. Discovering that this derivative of Fleming's bulb could now *amplify* electronic signals, he also sought a patent, despite the fact that he couldn't exactly explain how the effect worked. De Forest got his patent a year later, and used it to create an entirely new wireless communication system of his own. Fleming blew up, stating his invention had been "hijacked" by De Forest. A lengthy and ruinously expensive legal battle ensued. It was a battle Fleming eventually lost a few years later.

The oscillation valve and its derivatives were the central piece of technology used in electronics, until it was eventually superseded by the transistor decades later. In the meantime, it became the building block of long-distance telephony, of radar and television, and most importantly of all, computers.

THE SIDESTEP

Fleming's rags-to-not-quite-rags story is typical for almost every great genius who creates a breakthrough. That this happens so often is difficult to believe. We are conditioned by tales of the great inventors of history, those who got rich on the back of their world-changing products. Such stories are central to the capitalist dogma of our age: if you work hard enough, have enough talent, or strike just the right kind of luck, the market will reward you.

The market certainly did not look after Fleming. It did, however, look after the entrepreneurs who used the oscillation valve to create various technological advancements we all take for granted today. By 1920, for example, companies were making radio receivers that could be plugged into electric light sockets. Department stores ran exhibitions to show the devices, which could magically pull music and information straight out of the air. They sold like hotcakes.

Fleming did not imagine wireless transmissions as anything other than a replacement for the telegraph initially. It was actually De Forest, using his copy of Fleming's device, who created the first radio station, complete with the first broadcast radio commercial. De Forest's creation of broadcast radio entertainment is an example of a *sidestep*. With radio broadcasting, he took an existing capability to transmit individual messages point-to-point without wires, and moved it to a new market: providing news and entertainment for the masses. It was De Forest's sidestep that created mass media.

This kind of movement is the basic principle of the sidestep. You take existing, well understood capabilities into new areas where they can be used by new customers.

As you might imagine, there are numerous examples of sidesteps in all industries and countries, and we'll be examining some of the most famous later in this book. For now, however, it is enough to say that all of them involve doing one of two things: either disimproving or improving a product incrementally (we'll call this strategy dis/improvement from now on), or moving the product into an adjacent market altogether. Both are means of gaining additional market share for something working well already[1].

Let us examine, firstly, dis/improvement, a strategy that involves changing the set of features available at particular price points in order to adjust the price/performance ratio of the product.

Consider an airline, which often has multiple cabin classes on each plane, each with a different price. Now, the core product is transportation from place to place, and there is always some kind of basic version with very few extras. Probably, the airline offers just a meal and seat if it is a long haul flight, and less if the ride is very short. Here, the price/performance is balanced towards that minimum set of features necessary to move people around, and the price reflects that.

---

1   For students of innovation, much of the following discussion borrows heavily from the seminal work of Clayton Christensen, the innovation academic who first proposed a workable theory describing the mechanics of market disruption. His book *The Innovators Dilemma* is highly recommended.

Airlines, though, know there's another group of customers they can reach if they improve the product just a little bit. So they change the price/performance ratio: maybe there's a premium section, where the improvement represents a little extra legroom and perhaps superior food and beverages. In exchange for these additional features, an airline can charge a higher price. If the price increase is less than the perceived benefits of the better cabin, the airline has improved the price/performance ratio of their offer.

Of course, some airlines have taken a quite different approach to managing their price/performance ratio. Instead of making the cabin nicer, they've done everything possible to reduce price by removing features and downgrading. For most of us, flying is not a lovely experience. We're crammed in tiny seats, with barely-adequate meals, and it seems that the only point of differentiation is what has-been movie is playing on the screen on the back of the seat in front. That's if there is a screen at all.

Faced with significant disruption to their transport product by discount airlines (more on them in a moment), airlines have been forced to compete on price for customers who previously had little choice but to pay up if they wanted to reap the benefits of flying. Sometimes, in an attempt to differentiate, airlines have chosen to add bells and whistles that don't cost them anything extra, thereby improving their price/performance ratio "for free".

One of the airlines I most loved to fly with was Song, a subsidiary of Delta. It has now ceased flying as a separate entity, but was amongst the most innovative holiday airlines in the world. The defining feature of flying with Song – the thing that gave the airline its name, actually – was its practice of having the flight crew artistically interpret the safety demonstration to music. A safety demonstration complete with dancing and singing was something to behold, I can assure you. Not only did passengers actually pay attention, they usually clapped afterward.

Changing the price/performance curve of a product by

adding or removing features is one kind of sidestep. The other is tweaking product features so your existing capabilities are useful to entirely new markets altogether. Discount airlines are masters of the *move sidestep.*

The first discount airline was Southwest Airlines in the United States. It was an extremely disruptive entry to the airline market, because it did something no one had previously thought possible. Southwest decided it would target that portion of the travelling public who traditionally would have travelled by bus rather than flown. What is the difference between taking a bus and a plane? Apart from the cost, buses go point-to-point between individual city pairs. Aircraft, on the other hand, usually fly from regional airports to major cities, where you change planes to get to your destination. Airlines of any scale almost always operate this kind of hub-and-spoke model, because it ensures they can fill up their busiest routes (and biggest planes) with passengers they've flown in from smaller centres.

Hub-and-spoke has a downside, though, and that is you have to be able to move passengers and luggage between aircraft very efficiently. It has to be done with a very low error rate in an environment that's affected by truly ridiculous levels of unpredictability. Snowfall at Heathrow Airport? You might have thousands of missed connections to manage. Running hub-and-spoke airline infrastructure is expensive even when things go right. You can imagine the costs when things don't.

Southwest's business model was different. It wasn't going to operate hub-and-spoke. Instead, it would run unconnected flights between city pairs, just as bus companies did.

Consequently the company was able to eliminate a pretty significant portion of the infrastructure any other airline would have needed to operate the ground side at each airport.

Then, in order to reduce the cost of its seats still further, Southwest took away seat allocation, food services, and interconnects with other airlines. It also, latterly, forced customers to use online, self-service channels to buy tickets and check in. Taken together, these measures enabled the airline to match, and in some cases beat, the best price for travelling between city-pairs by bus. Customers flocked to airports. After all, why spend 10 hours in a bus, when a flight for the same amount of money could do the trip in a few hours?

Discount flying is a model that's been copied in most countries around the world since Southwest's initial success, to the great consternation (and considerable erosion of margins) of other airlines. One of the most famous international discount airlines is Irish carrier Ryan Air, who have taken the discount model to ridiculous extremes. In 2009, for example, it suggested it might soon put a coin slot in planes to charge for access to toilet facilities. It also said it had considered a "fat tax" for obese passengers and might, in future, require checked-in baggage to be carried by passengers to the aircraft. These more extreme measures have not yet materialised.

Though customers might not agree with Ryan Air's ruthless cost-cutting and aggressive customer service policy, the airline is a sensational example of a sidestep. It took the low cost model pioneered by Southwest and moved it to a European market then dominated by traditional carriers who were competing by adding features to their products – essentially a competition defined by the dis/improvement sidestep. Today, Ryan Air is the second largest airline in Europe. This growth rate is extraordinary considering its humble beginnings in 1985 – one propeller driven aircraft with 14 seats.

I'm certain readers are easily able to think of many other examples of sidesteps beyond the airline industry. The fact is, they're common everywhere, and for a good reason: they're not that difficult or complicated to execute. After all, the common feature of sidesteps is they take what is already working very well and tweak them just a bit. Tweaking things already known to be working is obviously much less risky than creating things from scratch, which is why sidesteps are so attractive to companies looking to increase their sales.

The upshot, though, is that wherever a sidestep is obvious, it is highly likely one has already occurred. Entering a crowded market with something that's not very different to what's already there is hardly a recipe for a hit product. How have companies addressed this issue when they sidestep? The answer is they've found ways to make their products better as more people use them. That way, every time they get a new customer, the chance of them getting the next one improves, too.

THE TWIST

What constitutes a *twist* exactly?

Let me begin to answer this question by giving you an example of a twist, one that will be very familiar to anyone who reads a newspaper on the way to work or at the weekends. Now, if you're the publisher of a newspaper, you know you have two groups of customers who must both be served differently if your publication is to be successful. On the one hand, there are readers, who pick up the paper for information and entertainment. And on the other, there are advertisers, who pay money to place advertisements, which they hope readers will notice and act on.

As the publisher, you're very aware that you must please advertisers to get the majority of your revenue. Pleasing them requires providing access to the best and largest group of readers. On the other hand, pleasing the reading customer group means giving them the best journalism money can buy. It is immediately obvious that in order to do *that*, as a newspaper owner, you have to retain the best advertisers to bring in as much income as possible.

Advertisers are the money side of a newspaper, and they are

disproportionately affected by the number of readers a paper has. If readership goes up, so does advertising revenue, so newspaper owners are highly motivated to subsidise the newsstand price to get more readers.

In the newspaper market, this has already reached the ultimate extreme: some newspapers are now completely free. Indeed, newspaper owners, in the battle to get the most readers, have now begun to employ people whose sole role is to give newspapers to readers as they walk past. When you add the cost of these people to the equation, newspaper publishers are now practically at the point of *paying* readers to read.

The rise of the free newspaper shows how twists work. Instead of constraining newspaper supply to sustain prices on the reader side, they work actively to expand consumption. Having the most readers is a hard-to-beat competitive advantage over everyone else, because the increase in advertising revenue funds competition on the *actual* battleground: creating the best content. In other words, the product gets better the more it is consumed.

Twists are therefore quite different to strategies companies have used to make money in the past: historically, almost all of them have been based on the concept of constraining supply. Traditional economics teaches us that goods are valuable if they are rare, so companies go out of their way to impose conditions that make them so. That's why firms have always cared about how many patents they hold, how many copyrights they've registered, and how many trade secrets they're protecting.

Those days are still with us, but increasingly, organisations have begun to work out that almost all the important constraints are actually on the *demand* side. They've recognised the important battleground is not building the best product, but building the best (and largest) customer base. Ultimately, that's what the twist is all about.

There are two broad variations of a twist. The first, which I call the *single twist*, operates in circumstances where increasing consumption makes a product more desirable without modifying the price/performance curve.

Let me give you an example that illustrates how this works. In July 1995, *Business Week* magazine reported that management authors Michael Treacy and Fred Wiersema had managed to get their new business book onto the *New York Times* Best Seller List by buying 50,000 copies of their own work from bookshops. The bookstores they chose happened to be the ones whose sales figures the *Times* monitored to construct their list in the first place. Even when the pair stopped buying books, their title stayed on the list.

This is an example of a single twist where increasing consumption made the over all proposition of the book better. Everyone believed the book worthy of reading because everyone *else* seemed to be buying it. Did the price/performance ratio of the book change? Hardly. But demonstrable consumption of the book made it sell anyway, *despite* the fact it was apparently not that good, if reviewers were to be believed.

Single twists accelerate demand without changing the price/performance ratio of a product. *Double twists*, on the other hand, accelerate demand *and* change the price/performance at the same time.

A good example of a successful double twist is the rise of the fax machine, a device enabling two parties to send documents over telephone lines. Here, there are two groups of customers: senders and receivers. The basic functionality of the machine is dependent on both customer groups having send and receive capability. Clearly, it isn't very useful to have a fax machine if the person you wish to send a document to doesn't have one. On the other hand, every time one of your associates gets a machine, the over all value of *your* machine increases, because you can send to more people. As more people got fax machines, not only were they more useful to users; peer pressure made it more certain you would *want* to get one. Miss out on an important, time-critical business document because you were the only one who couldn't receive it? No thank you.

These are double twists where the inherent value of a product increases as the number of users increase. But double twists work just as well when indirect value increases with consumption. Indirect value occurs when increasing consumption of a product creates a subsidiary market of products and services. Video game consoles are an excellent example.

What is the *real* business in consoles? It isn't the machines themselves, which are often sold at a loss. It is, instead, on the games side where all the money is made. One estimate put the total value of the market in 2010 at US$51.7 billion[2]. It is a market that is creeping up on the value of the *entire* movie industry.

What induces a studio to publish a game on a particular console? Obviously, the answer is they build their games for the platform where the largest number of players is available. Therefore, if you are the manufacturer of a console, you have an inherent motivation to get as many players as possible using your machine. This motivation is usually expressed in terms of *subsidies* for the gaming console. The subsidy helps expand game consumption, and is usually supported by some kind of game-tax: publishers have to pay the console manufacturer a royalty on every game they sell.

GOOGLE'S SIDESTEP AND TWIST

Now that we have a preliminary understanding of the sidestep and twist, let us turn to a recent case that's been playing out in real life: Google's foray into GPS systems and turn-by-turn

---

2   Strategy Analytics, May 26, 2011: "Global Video Game Forecast: 2011"

navigation. Google has been interested in maps for years. It launched its first version of Google Maps in 2005, which was based on the work of an Australian company called Where2 Technologies, which it acquired the year before. At launch, Google Maps showed road maps only. What was good about the service, though, was it enabled you to create specific driving directions between two locations, complete with important points of interest along the way, such as hotels. This additional information came from extensive information Google was already indexing about places and things to do as part of its main search business.

By the middle of 2005, Google had expanded Maps to include "hybrid" views incorporating satellite photography superimposed onto the basic map. Now, customers had the option to see where they were going "from the air". In the years that followed, further features were added, including two of particular note to us at the moment: real time traffic and Street View, both of which were launched in 2007.

The former, Traffic, uses real time data sourced from local traffic management authorities to colour the roads on maps depending on how quickly traffic is moving. So, for example, roads coloured green have fast moving traffic, whilst ones with jams and snarls are coloured bright red.

Street View, launching the same year as Traffic, was somewhat more controversial. Using specially modified cars with roof-mounted 360 degree cameras, Google drove up and down every road it could find in every supported country, taking panoramic snap shots every few meters. These images were incorporated into its maps, enabling users to "fly down" to street level and pan around as if they were actually standing there.

By 2008, Google Maps was the fourth most popular service the company offered, running behind Search, Gmail and YouTube.

Google decided to sidestep. In this case, Google sidestepped from a web service aimed solely at users of traditional computers, to a mobile service aimed at those who ordinarily would have relied on paper maps, or more interestingly, a conventional GPS navigation unit. The announcement that Google would add this feature to its then new Android mobile operating system came in 2009. It would be free, and come as part of every handset sold from then on.

Markets reacted instantly, wiping almost a billion US dollars from the valuation of the two dominant GPS players in the industry, TomTom and Garmin. Markets always react badly against incumbents when big players like Google, Microsoft and Apple decide to enter a product category. Usually though, initial market fear, uncertainty and doubt is tempered when it becomes clear that the entrants have a way to go to match the execution of incumbents.

But the problem for Garmin and TomTom was *their* competitive advantage was built on the quality (and control) of their map data, which they repackaged in various devices to make a profit. When you are building turn-by-turn navigation software, much of the cost comes from a special data set you need to incorporate with maps: detailed, road level information about markings, turning conditions and traffic restrictions. To create this information, you have few choices but to drive the roads themselves on a regular basis, noting important features in a database.

The first two companies to create such a database, sometime in the late 1980s, were TeleAtlas and Navteq. Both companies created their initial data sets by hiring people carrying a dictaphone to describe important features at multiple points as they drove every road of importance in each supported country. As GPS systems weren't generally available at the time this was first done, the measurements were taken by dead reckoning with the support of a gyro compass.

These early databases were very valuable, and both companies developed substantial businesses based on licensing their information to manufacturers of an emerging product category

– navigation devices for cars. They were valuable for another reason, of course: the cost in creating a competitive database was very, very large. You'd need large teams of people in each city the database was to support, and the work never stopped. Streets and driving conditions change all the time.

For most companies, it was much less expensive just to licence the data. At the beginning, this was true even for Google, who used licenced data in its first maps product. Google's decision to create Street View changed this, however. It was already driving every street to get its panoramic photography, so adding local turn-by-turn data was not much extra effort. By October 2009, the company had a sufficiently large database they were able to announce the termination of their agreement with TeleAtlas, and soon after announced their own GPS navigation system.

Because Google was no longer reliant on licensing the expensive turn-by-turn data set, a zero price point suddenly not only became possible, but made sense in the context of Google's more traditional businesses.

Google doesn't really care about charging for content, whether that is turn-by-turn navigation data or any other kind. It prefers, instead, to sell your *attention* to advertisers in payment for organising content dynamically in a way that keeps you coming back time after time. Whether or not it actually owns the content is less important than whether it can organise it for you at a cost at which advertising can be profitable.

On the Android platform, Google's GPS product is quite different to that of everyone else. Firstly, it relies on a data connection at all times, since it loads its information from Google's servers when needed, rather than storing it locally. As a result, the data sets it utilises are much more extensive than those embedded into any console-mounted device, and the data is always up-to-date.

For example, when you come close to your destination on Google's navigation tool, the view automatically switches to Street View so you have panoramic images of where you're going at a street level. No one else can do that. Secondly, Google has a database of everything. The database is content created by end users – essentially all the web pages in the world. If a blog talks about a particular service or product, that information can be found via the Android GPS system. If someone has uploaded a photograph from a particular place and shared it, that information is available. And, of course, most businesses are highly motivated to have their company details up-to-date in Google's indexes, because that provides them with traffic for their businesses.

In other words, users, of their own volition, deepen the depth and quality of Google's database. They increase its value every time they consume more of the mapping product.

You can see the problem for Garmin and TomTom. Firstly, they have no way of getting Street View data, since that's something Google has built exclusively for their own web product. NavTech and TeleAtlas don't do web products themselves, so don't have street pictures. Then, too, neither company is a search engine. They don't have the world's users updating their database of interesting places for them. Instead, they have to buy datasets such as government postcode databases, which usually lag reality in terms of accuracy.

WHAT'S NEXT?

You will by now have a taste of what the rest of this book is about, which can be summarised in three key observations on successful modern-day products.

The first observation is this: great breakthrough inventions, the ones that create first-of capabilities never before seen, practically never make much money. Fleming is a case in point. If we believe capitalist mythology, he should have made billions on his patent for the first electronic device. He didn't. Really successful products have big ecosystems that surround them: sales, manufacturing, distribution and all the other apparatus of real business that makes an invention an economic proposition by improving the price/performance ratio. Breakthroughs, on the other hand, are usually not commercialised in a mature way.

The second observation is that old style competitive barriers (patents, copyrights and so forth) aren't nearly as effective as they once were. These days, it is much more effective to create competitive barriers in the form of twists – situations where competitors find themselves confronted with products that users make better the more they use them.

The final observation is this: over the last decade or so, more hit products have occurred when companies have taken a sidestep and added a twist than any other strategy.

GETTING CUSTOMERS IN

....

CHAPTER TWO

Fleming with his oscillation valve and Google with its Android turn-by-turn navigation application are examples of the mechanics of the sidestep. In the former case, Fleming's breakthrough created the basis for an industry. Despite this, Fleming made very little from his invention.

Google's turn-by-turn navigation, on the other hand, wasn't a breakthrough at all. Instead, it incorporated products it had already got working well into a new form factor, and in the process changed the parameters for the rest of the industry. Stories similar to that of Google are repeated in almost all industries and product categories.

This begs a question, though. Why is it companies who copy things already working well seem to make more money than those who invest in genuine research that leads to breakthrough innovation?

To answer this question, it is useful to examine some of the biggest selling products and services over the last couple of decades. As you can see in Table 2.1, every one is practically a household name.

Category	Product	Sales	Precedents
Literature	*Harry Potter* series	> 400 Million Copies	Inspired by British boarding school tradition and derivative fantasy
Medicines	Lipitor	US$12.5 billion per annum	Fifth drug in the statin class to reach the market
Automotive	Volkswagen Beetle	21 million units	"Borrowed" many of the features of the now unknown Tatra, a car developed in Nazi Germany
Film	*Gone with the Wind*	US$1.6 billion in total takings (in today's money)	Based on the best-selling, Pulitzer Prize-winning book by Margaret Mitchell
Personal computer	Commodore 64	17 million units	An incremental improvement on an earlier design by Commodore (the Vic-20) which was also a best-seller
Alcoholic beverage	Guinness	10 million pints a day	The Stout is an Irish version of the popular English Porter beer, which preceded Guinness
Music	*Thriller*, by Michael Jackson	120 million units	The music video, which jump-started sales in the second year, brought movie-quality production to music
Online search	Google	US$24.4 billion	An incremental improvement on previous search engines such as AltaVista and Yahoo
Social network	Facebook	US$2 billion (est)	Preceded by MySpace and SixDegrees.com
Mobile phone	Nokia 1100	250.1 million units	Similar to three best-selling Nokia models that preceded it

Table 2.1: Big Hits in Recent Times

It is the last column in Table 2.1 that's most interesting, since it reveals that in not one single case was there a genuine breakthrough for each of these hit products and services.

Take, for example, the case of Michael Jackson's *Thriller*, the best selling music album of all time by a long margin. Now, arguably, *Thriller* represents the creative apex of Jackson's career, but that doesn't explain how an album of just nine songs stayed at the number one spot in the charts for 37 weeks and had 80 consecutive weeks in the top 10. The only record that's ever exceeded its charting performance was the soundtrack to the movie, *West Side Story*, some 30 years before.

When *Thriller* was released at the end of 1982 it was immediately successful. Seven of the nine tracks were released as singles, and all of them made it to the top 10 on the charts. Though this would have been a stellar performance in anyone's estimation, the real magic of *Thriller* was yet to come.

By the summer of 1983, the album had begun to slide. Jackson, reputedly, rang his record company executives demanding they do something to boost sales. The response was standard record industry marketing: make another music video from one of the tracks on the album.

Jackson knew just another music video wasn't going to cut it. Sales were slowing for a reason, and it was because the public was getting tired of the content, the nine songs on the album. New content was the answer. Content so compelling it would kick-start the record into a second run at the top.

The sidestep that followed was brilliant: bring the magic of the movies to music video. Prior to the video for *Thriller*, music videos were mainly visual eye-candy featuring the artists singing and playing their instruments in various settings. They were an essential component of the success of any new single in the 1980s, when MTV was rising as a primary medium for music videos. As the "MTV generation" emerged, the music video was the only way to access a market moving away from radio.

All the major artists of the 1980s, names such as Madonna and Duran Duran, quickly became skilful at creating music videos using newly available low-cost production techniques. Jackson, too, used similar techniques for the first videos for *Thriller.*

For the album's title track, though, Jackson decided not to do "budget", and instead retained a renowned feature-length movie director using his own money. His director demanded – and got – all the trappings of a big-budget feature, which included 10 cameras and dozens of extras. By the time they were finished, *Thriller* was the most expensive music video ever produced.

The final product is 14 minutes long and is more short film than music video. It tells the story of a young man who takes a girl on an outing to the theatre. The movie they're seeing is a horror, complete with zombies and werewolves. When they leave the theatre, the movie turns into reality, with Jackson himself turning into a zombie. The story concludes when the principal characters awaken to find it has all been a dream, though the yellow gleam in Jackson's eye in the closing sequence makes us doubt whether it was in fact a dream or not.

Such a complex story line – coupled with cinema quality production and the professional direction of a real feature-length moviemaker was completely unprecedented. The result was a sensation. MTV, who premiered the video, had to play it two times an hour to keep up with demand. A complimentary product, the home video cassette, *The Making of Michael Jackson's Thriller* was, at its peak, the top-selling home video release of all time, and sold nine million copies.

Thriller is not unique amongst successful products. Every one listed in Table 2.1 is the result of a sidestep from something else. But they all have another characteristic as well: their sidesteps all came from products with significant existing demand.

Guinness is the world's best-selling beer, and over 10 million pints a day are poured of the famous dark ale. It has a long history, spanning several hundred years, starting with Irishman

Arthur Guinness, who began making the product after 20 years
brewing more conventional brews. It is popularly believed that
Guinness invented the Stout, as the product variety is known,
but this is incorrect. As with all sidesteps, the drink was actually
a minor change from a style of beer already very popular: the
British Porter, which emerged in London some time after 1721.
Porter beers are historically important because they were the
first to be aged at the brewery. Before the Porter, manufacturers
dispatched the product straight after brewing to pubs, either to
be aged onsite or by the publican's dealer. Porters consequently
became famous for the consistent colour and taste they offered.

Brewery-based ageing led to the realisation that mass-
produced beer could be an economic success if sufficiently large
volumes were achieved. Some breweries concentrated on various
technological improvements that allowed this, and in the process
achieved huge commercial windfalls. Leading the charge were
the Porter breweries, who remained the kings of beer production
for almost 150 years.

Arthur Guinness didn't create anything new with his version
of the Porter, but did "improve" the product by mixing aged
brew with freshly brewed beer to create a sharp lactic flavour
to the finished product. The incremental taste change proved
a market success. By the time Arthur Guinness died in 1803,
his brewery was outputting over 20,000 barrels a year, and he'd
stopped producing all other varieties. Much of the commercial
success can be attributed to the existence of prior demand for
the Porter variety.

For every product in Table 2.1, this kind of incremental
change supported by previous demand seems to be a key feature
of success. The question is, why?

S-CURVES AND THE PSYCHOLOGY OF DEMAND

For an answer, we need to examine how new ideas spread. Many people mistakenly believe people adopt new ideas the moment they hear about them. According to this thinking, information about something new arrives, maybe from a mass-market campaign on television or print media, and potential adopters make a value judgement for themselves about whether there is any point in trying it for themselves. This is the model that drives much modern day marketing.

Campaigns are started to get messages to as many people as possible, often using mass media or other one-to-many mechanisms. Slightly more sophisticated approaches target specific demographics, industries, or interest groups in the hope of ensuring the messages are interesting to as many people as possible.

All this activity is supposed to generate a certain number of leads, which in turn, convert into a smaller number of sales. In this very traditional approach to marketing, one expands the amount of advertising in order to expand the value of the sales pipeline.

When you execute marketing in this way, you'll likely find it works reasonably well for products with which potential buyers are familiar. Washing detergent, for example, is a product category with which everyone has more than passing acquaintance, at least if they want to ensure their friends and colleagues can stand being in the same room with them.

Now, when an ordinary buyer of washing powder sees an advertisement for a new product, he or she is able to evaluate the relative advantages involved in switching based on their own experience. They decide to buy depending on their personal circumstances and whether the new option appeals to them or not.

But imagine for a moment you are responsible for washing

the clothes in a country that doesn't have running water, washing machines or electricity. Soap, if it is used at all, is hand-made and probably something of a luxury. Suddenly, you see the same advertisement for washing powder, an innovation completely unprecedented in your experience. Your response is to discount the advertisement immediately.

The problem is that you have no previous understanding of washing with powder. In fact, you probably can't even see how the new powder fits into your mental model of washing clothes, given the likelihood powder will get washed away by the stream you're using for water before you can get anything clean with it in the first place. Washing powder is only useful if you know about washing machines. And the only way you're going to really understand such devices is by observing other people getting the benefit from using one.

The inherent problem with breakthroughs is no one really understands them until someone else they trust tries them out. This is the reason most hit products have lots of precedents which people recognise. It is also the reason so many hits are derived from inventions already well in demand in the market place.

The importance of leveraging existing demand into new categories has been understood for decades. One of the most remarkable scholars of our age was a man named Everett Rogers, amongst the first to study the way new ideas spread. Even today, he's relatively unknown, but his work has become stupendously important because he's the man who first worked out the dynamics of social networks. Social networks, in the last decade and a bit, have become one of the principle drivers of value on the internet.

But in 1952, when Rogers finished his undergraduate degree, very few people had actually begun thinking about the mechanisms people used to communicate with each other about their ideas. The mass media marketing model I described earlier was king, and with good reason: anyone with enough money to get out a message about any product to a wide enough market was able to make huge returns.

But Rogers was confused by developments closer to home, in a farming community in Iowa. Landowners there were delaying the introduction of agricultural innovations for years, even though these might be economically beneficial to them. Why didn't they just change their methods?

Ten years earlier, scholars had examined the way Iowa corn growers reacted to news of hybrid seeds. The new seeds offered about a 20% increase in yield, but it wasn't until almost a decade later everyone was routinely planting the new varieties. The interesting thing was, despite the demonstrable benefits of planting hybrid seeds, very few farmers did so at the beginning.

However, towards the end of the decade there was an explosion in their use.

Academics looked at this interesting adoption pattern more closely and came to the conclusion that most farmers ignored any positive messages about new seeds until they could see evidence from their neighbours that they actually worked. Rogers' contribution was noticing this didn't happen *only* with seed corn. He encountered the same effect in the roll out of kindergarten schools, the spread of antibiotic drugs and in methods of driving instruction.

In fact, he concluded, every time a brand new idea came along it exhibited exactly the same characteristics. Ideas started with a very slow take off and adoption increased only slowly during the first few periods. Eventually, however, adoption reached a critical point where enough people were using the new thing that everyone else started copying.

What Rogers recognised was if you plot the number of people adopting a new idea against time, you get an S-shaped curve of the kind shown in Figure 2.1.

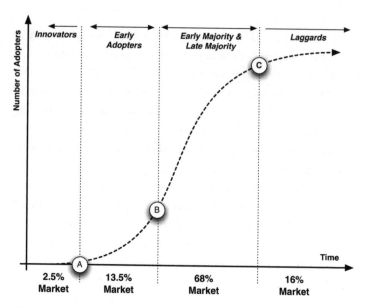

Figure 2.1: Adoption S-curves

At the beginning (point A), there are very few people who will take any kind of risk on a truly new product. Those few, very few, people who do, have particular reasons for doing so. Maybe they are gamblers and like to take unusual risks. Perhaps they're sufficiently wealthy that they don't care if their new product or service doesn't work the way they expect. Or, maybe, they have their backs against the wall and try whatever it is out of desperation. In the figure, they are the group known as innovators, and according to Rogers' research, comprise about 2.5% of any given market.

Now whatever the reason for their behaviour, innovators are the only group who will make the leap to try something unprecedented. Everyone else needs reassurance from one or more third parties before they'll commit. Where does this reassurance come from? For most, it is from trusted colleagues and friends who have already tried the innovation.

Now, if you look at your own circle of trusted associates, you'll likely notice they all have multiple things in common with you. This is not an accident: we tend to trust only those who are similar to us. The more pronounced the differences between people, the less likely they are to develop a relationship in the first place.

This explains the dynamic of the S-curve. If we say the only people who will try out something new are those a bit different from the mainstream, and everyone else will only adopt if they see someone else who's similar to them doing so first, it follows that at the start you'll have hardly any success at all.

You have to drive the idea by pumping the market with messages, and ideally, by targeting those specific individuals who are most likely to adopt the new thing. Initially, they are so different from everyone else that there is little or no effect. But eventually, you start to reach people who are slightly nearer the average. Somewhere between point A and B in Figure 2.1, those people are engaging with the product. This is the group known as "early adopters", and in most markets, they comprise about 13.5% of the total.

Now, these slightly more mainstream people might not implicitly trust everything they see the innovators doing, but at least there is some evidence for them to look at. A percentage is willing to at least give the new thing a go.

Eventually, this influencing process reaches enough people that the more general demographic can see evidence that it works. By point B, the idea has reached a point of "critical mass", and sales take off whether or not the vendor pumps the market with messages. At this point all the early adopters are using the new innovation, and they've influenced a new group – the "early majority" – to adopt as well.

The early majority, typically, represent somewhere in the order of about 34% of a market. They are slightly less risk averse than average, so they're willing to try the new product if they've had positive messages from the early adopters.

Yet even now, not everyone is willing to take a chance.

Another 34% of the market is composed of the "late majority", who have to see positive success with the product from someone they trust in the early majority before they'll try it themselves. A majority of them will have done so by the time the curve gets to point C, the point at which growth begins to slow.

At point C, all that's left is a market segment known as "the laggards": those in a market who are so risk averse they're not willing to change to the new product unless they're almost *forced* to do so. By the time a product has reached point C, it is nearly dead, because it has run out of viable customers. Laggards comprise about 16% of the total market.

You can, therefore, see the importance of the sidestep, which can kick a product into markets where there are new customers.

The S-curve provides us with an insight which is critically important when talking about introducing genuinely new products: to get a sale with any particular customer you have to get some, or all, of the people that the customer trusts to buy as well. As you might expect, this can be difficult: there is often a chicken-and-egg problem to overcome. No one will be the first to buy, so no one buys at all.

Let us now return to the sidestep and the reason it is such a powerful driver of success. As I described a moment ago, the hit products listed in Table 2.1 were all based on other commercial successes. The S-curve explains why: you need to have significant numbers of people familiar with a concept if you want them to adopt something new and existing demand for an existing product or service provides that.

When you make a sidestep, you are adopting the S-curve for another product and applying it to your own. The result is a shortcut that eliminates the need for exhaustive marketing targeting the "out-there" innovators. Everyone already has experience with the product category or technology, so they can make a decision without the need for much evidence from people they trust. In other words, you're introducing a new kind of washing powder, rather than washing powder as well as the machines needed to wash with it.

PRICE/PERFORMANCE AND THE ECONOMICS OF BREAKTHROUGHS

The S-curve doesn't account for everything we can observe about the rise of new products and services, however. If everything was about S-curves, then it ought to be possible to take genuine breakthroughs and market the hell out of them to achieve success. The S-curve suggests all that's necessary to guarantee success is reaching enough people in the innovator segment with a resonant message. They, in turn, will lead everyone else to adopting in simple stages.

But if this were true, then some of the most hyped inventions in history should have sold like hotcakes. Take, for example, the Segway Personal Transportation device, unveiled to an ultra-expectant world on 3 December 2001 on the ABC News morning programme, *Good Morning America.* The device – an unusual and innovative self-balancing scooter – had been subject to months of frenzied speculation prior to launch.

"It", as everyone nicknamed the project prior to the unveiling, was to be "more important than the internet" according to one leading venture capitalist. Jeff Bezos, founder of Amazon, opined: "cities would be built around [it]". Even the late Steve Jobs of Apple Computer fame said the machine would be as big as the personal computer. At least he said so in public, though subsequent disclosures have indicated that privately he felt "it sucked".

When the machine came out, the over all media reaction was more "huh?" than "wow!" "It's a scooter", some complained, prompting Segway's investor to say, "It won't beam you to Mars or turn lead into gold. So sue me!" Despite the hype, which included images of ex-President George Bush falling off one on YouTube, the product has not been commercially very successful.

Initially, the launch sales target for Segway was 40,000 units per year, and the company expected it would sell between 50,000 and 100,000 units in the first 13 months. However, by 2007, only 30,000 units had been sold, and the device has never revolutionised personal transportation in cities in the way expected.

Segway itself has been close-mouthed about its performance, and there is much speculation as to whether the company has yet to turn a profit. After all, it spent close to US$100 million developing its personal transport technology, and that kind of investment takes time to recoup. Segway is a travel machine that has remained an ultra-niche option despite the huge mind share it has generated over the last decade.

But, if S-curves worked as advertised, a small group of adopters should have immediately taken up the Segway, convincing others to adopt as well over time. That has obviously not happened, so we must look further than the social dynamics represented by S-curves to find an explanation.

For a more complete explanation of the failure of some innovations in spite of huge mind share, we need to examine the *economics* of breakthroughs, as well as the way society encounters them.

The story of the mechanisation of transportation, which began with the steam engine, sidestepped into railways, and ended up with the internal combustion engine is an excellent historical case of this occurring. Let us turn now to seventeenth-century England, a land with an economy based entirely on the application of human labour to production. This was a time when mechanisation was extremely limited, being coupled geographically to those places with running water or good wind energy. Natural motive forces were all that were available, so if you needed a machine to do work, you had to build it close to these local power sources, which were in short supply. For an engine anywhere else, you used animals or men. The price of acquiring such labour was the key defining input to the cost of everything.

The critical thought that initiated the transition from this bucolic society was the realisation that steam could be made to do useful work. Earliest records suggest this idea first occurred in ancient Greece. Heron of Alexandria, a prolific inventor and mathematician, created a thing called an Aeolipile, whose basic design was a sealed container with two jet outlets. By mounting the container on a rotating base and applying heat to create steam, the jets were capable of moving the whole apparatus. Heron, employing similar principals, then created a mechanised way of opening temple doors by condensing steam in a bucket, the weight of which was linked by pulleys and ropes to the door itself. Over time, the bucket got heavy enough to pull the doors open by force of gravity.

Heron went on to create many other novel devices of limited practical utility, including the world's first vending machine, capable of dispensing holy water on the deposit of a coin in a slot. This invention is now applied, in refined form, to the new holy water of today, the soft drink. But steam, as a practical engine for doing real work, remained an unrealised possibility.

It was almost two millennia later when a British military engineer examined the possibilities of steam again. Thomas Savery, born in 1650, was the first to register a patent for a machine that could remove a little water from flooded mines by condensing steam.

It was a vast improvement on the steam condensation apparatus Heron used to mechanically open doors, but was nonetheless hopelessly inefficient. Every pumping action required both the heating and cooling of the water in the chamber, so the machine was ruinously expensive fuel-wise. Nonetheless, Savery went on to install his engines in a small number of mines where the economics made sense. At the start, the conditions where this was the case were quite extreme.

To be more effective than human or animal labour, the mine

had to be shallow (since the engine was incapable of raising water from depths of more than about 12 meters) had to be subject to flooding, and be either a coal mine itself, or situated closely enough to some other source of fuel that transportation costs were negligible. The business case for installing a Savery engine was usually very difficult. Nonetheless, the engine was a breakthrough – it was the first occasion that mechanical labour had successfully substituted for natural or animal sources.

Just over a decade after Savery, the next great efficiency increase in mechanical power arrived. In 1712, an ironmonger, Thomas Newcomen (1664–1729), eliminated the boil-condense cycle used by Savery by having a piston, separate from the generation of steam, act as the condenser.

Newcomen's new design delivered a significant increase in efficiency and safety. Overnight, mines which had previously become unworkable due to flooding became viable again. Compared to the Savery engine, much less fuel was needed to lift a gallon of water. Furthermore, the engine could work with much deeper mines.

Even Newcomen's improvements, however, did not give steam engines economics that made them suitable for deployment beyond their limited applications in pumping mines. Certainly, they were wholly unsuitable for building the moving transports that would later reshape the world.

At this point, steam engines were massive. They needed to be in order to make their vacuum mechanic work at a useful scale. Their size meant even if it had been possible to make the engines efficient enough, there was no chance at all they could ever be attached to a moving object.

The great efficiency that enabled engines to get smaller was pioneered by the famous James Watt (1736–1819), who finally separated the boil and condense cycle completely. By 1769, he'd achieved the most powerful engine the world had ever seen, and it was powerful and efficient enough that the inventor was able to scale back its size without limiting the uses to which it could be put. With Watt, steam engines began to find a use beyond mining. The reason was his kind of engine was now efficient enough that the economics made sense, even when limited fuel transportation costs were added.

It was around this time that the industrial revolution kicked off in earnest, driven in part by the application of Watt's engines to automatic cotton mills. However, whilst steam power continued to expand as its economics improved, adoption beyond a factory setting continued to elude it.

The main problem was no longer one of fuel cost, but reliability. The manufacture of steam engines as the eighteenth century drew to a close was highly capital-intensive. Each engine was unique, a craftsman's interpretation of the plans provided by Watt's company. As a result, maintenance was expensive and required exceptionally skilled labour, usually from the team that built the engine in the first place. In the end, these early steam engines worked only about half the time, making them very expensive indeed.

Taking reliability into account, after almost 100 years of development, steam was still an inferior alternative to wind or hydropower. This is obvious from the data in Table 2.2, which compares steam use to the other dominant power sources of the day, wind and water.

Year	Steam	Water	Wind
1760	5,000	70,000	10,000
1800	35,000	120,000	15,000
1830	160,000	160,000	20,000
1870	2060,000	230,000	10,000
1907	9659,000	178,000	5,000

Table 2.2: Units of Horsepower Provided by Type, 1760–1907 [3]

---

3   Kanefsky, J.W. "The Diffusion of Power Technology in British Industry, 1760–1870." Ph.D thesis, University of Exeter (1979).

In the four decades succeeding the first engine by Savery, steam power remained relatively underused compared to wind and water sources. However, by 1800, steam had increased its output contribution seven fold, and overtaken wind power in terms of total horsepower produced. Steam may still have been an order of magnitude less important than water, but during the next 30 years, this situation was to reverse itself. Sometime around 1830, steam just took off, eclipsing all other power sources. It will be no strain on the deductive powers of anyone to work out why: it was around 1830 that locomotion powered by steam engines finally became a reality.

What was the innovation that changed the game so suddenly? Watt's engines, though hugely more efficient than anything that preceded them, were still massive, and far too big to move around. The problem was inventors were at the limits of the efficiency they could reasonably achieve so long as they used steam at atmospheric pressure. They needed high-pressure steam, but the materials available to Watt and his contemporaries made this a very dangerous proposition. Any fault in the manufacturing of the boiler, or more likely the pipes, would likely result in a deathly explosion.

By the start of the nineteenth century, some of these dangers had receded with advances in material science and engineering. Cautiously, inventors started to examine what they might do with engines operating on pressurised steam. Leading the charge was the United Kingdom's Richard Trevithick (1771–1883).

Trevithick was the son of a mine captain, so he was familiar with the earlier generation of steam engines. Watching them day-in and day-out made enough of an impression that he decided to follow an engineering career himself. His experiments with high pressure steam, when they finally worked, showed him that his engines had the potential to be not only an order of magnitude more efficient, but also much, much smaller.

In 1801, Trevithick demonstrated the superiority of his

design by mounting an engine on wheels, and used it to convey several men up the road to a nearby village. This event was the first time *transportation* by steam was ever accomplished, though the machine ran out of steam too quickly to be anything more than a demonstration.

By 1803, Trevithick had resolved this problem and put his next generation design on wheels as well, naming the new device the "London Steam Carriage". By driving it from London's Paddington to Holborn and back (some three miles), he proved that effective transportation was possible without horses.

As a demonstration it was effective, but unfortunately, Trevithick suffered the age-old economic problem mechanised power had always had until then – cheaper alternatives were readily available. For potential customers of the London Steam Carriage, once the initial thrill of being moved by machine was over, it was much less expensive (and much less dirty) to revert to horse and carriage.

Trevithick was not deterred. One year later, he mounted another of his engines on a track-borne vehicle in a coal mine that had, till then, been operated by horse. It was able to move a load of 10 tons of ore, 80 men, and five extra wagons a distance of nine miles. Furthermore, it did so faster than an equivalent team of horses could have done it. Finally, Trevithick had a success, though his invention was still uneconomical because the machines, the fuel and the men needed to take care of them were about the same price as using human and animal labour alone.

More improvements were needed. The next major figure in the tale of steam is George Stephenson (1781–1848). His contribution to steam power was incremental in nature: he made engines that were a little smaller and more efficient. Stephenson's engines tipped the economic balance because they were finally cheaper to operate than using horses and men.

To prove the point, in 1825 Stephenson convinced the owners of the soon-to-open Stockton and Darlington Railway in the United Kingdom to use his engines in addition to horses. His engines were able to pull much greater loads than the horses and it soon became obvious the railway could run much longer, much faster trains if it dispensed with horses altogether.

Interest in railways exploded when Stephenson, five years later, opened a line between Manchester and Liverpool designed expressly to carry passengers rather than cargo. Thereafter, demand for steam power expanded quickly. Steam had reached a point where it was *finally* economic enough to be used by a large number of adopters, which triggered the critical mass point on the adoption S-curve.

Before the railway, the world was one kind of place – bucolic and pastoral. Afterwards, it began to take the shape of the industrialised world we are now familiar with. It is a transition that was driven by constant refinements of a breakthrough's economics until they make sense for a large audience of adopters.

The economic dynamics we've just explored in the historical development of steam occurs in every industry. What usually happens is a breakthrough is introduced, but initially it has limited real applicability because its economics don't make sense. Over time, efficiency and cost improves, which makes the breakthrough possible for larger groups of people to actually adopt. This is illustrated in Figure 2.2 (following page).

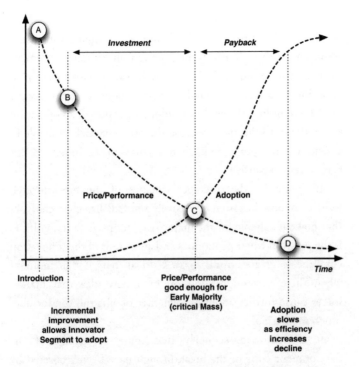

Figure 2.2: The Price/Performance of Innovations and S-curves

At point A, when the breakthrough first appears, it is very expensive to utilise. The number of potential adopters, if any, is tiny, because the circumstances in which the breakthrough makes sense economically are extremely limited. However, multiple generations of improvements follow quickly.

By point B, the breakthrough has a price/performance point good enough for the innovator segment of a particular market to make economic use of it. The usual dynamics of the S-curve then start, driven by increasing efficiencies of the innovation. These efficiencies get better over time as new introductions and improvements come along.

For the vendor of an initial breakthrough, though, the time between point B and point C is unlikely to be very profitable. Firstly, any investment in initial development must now be recovered and these costs will not be insignificant. More importantly, though, this is the time that maximum investment in marketing is required. As we saw in the previous section, if adoption is to occur, the market must be flooded with messages in order to induce the vital early adopter portion of a population to try the breakthrough. Because the only channels available to a vendor at this point are likely to be mass media in nature, this can be very expensive.

By point C, the price/performance of the breakthrough (which by now has been extensively refined) has characteristics that make it suitable for the majority of adopters to try. Point C is the position where economics and awareness of the innovation combine to create critical mass. Critical mass is that moment when there is enough adoption of a new idea that market forces cause further adoption, whether or not the vendor does much marketing.

It is, furthermore, likely that some percentage of the development costs of the breakthrough have been recovered by this point. Consequently, point C is also the time at which a vendor begins to make really significant money from their efforts.

There is a one final point in the figure – point D – that we must now consider. That's the point at which the improvement in price/performance of a breakthrough begins to decelerate. When that happens, it usually triggers vendors, who are no longer making the windfall profits their initial sidestep generated, to try new things in order to maintain their growth. If another sidestep is available, they will usually take this route.

The sidestep, when it occurs, will often implement a new technology or process to kick start a price/performance curve with economics good enough to attract any new customer groups. If that's not possible, firms will then try to sidestep their existing price/performance curve to a new market altogether (a move sidestep) in order to reach brand new customers. They will most likely have little choice in doing this: pressure from shareholders on managers is significant when those in authority imagine that growth is slowing. What happens if neither of these options are available? The answer is simple: firms cut prices.

This is a topic to which we'll return in the next chapter, since it is the purpose of the twist to prevent this from happening. But for now, let us compare the theoretical model of Figure 2.2 to the actual data for steam engine efficiency and adoption, shown in Figure 2.3. As you can see, the curves are the shapes we'd expect.

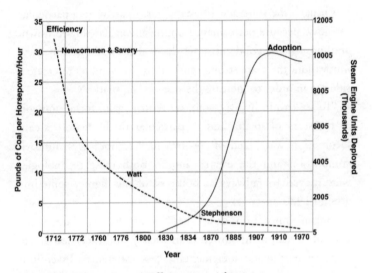

Figure 2.3: Steam Engine Efficiency vs. Adoption [4]

Steam engines started out with very poor economics, as reflected by the amount of coal needed to generate a horsepower hour of work. Things rapidly improved, however, and as they did so, adoption of the technology increased. Eventually, by the time of Trevithick, the economics of steam improved to a degree that it made sense for large numbers of machines to be built. Coupled

---

4   Dr. Grant Walker. "Engine Efficiency Adoption Statistics". University of Calgary.

with the work of Stephenson, who made the move sidestep to turn steam engines into commercial steam locomotives, we begin to see the S-shaped curve take off somewhere after 1830.

THE BREAKTHROUGH – SIDESTEP – BREAKTHROUGH CYCLE

Point D on Figure 2.2 (and reflected between 1910 and 1970 in Figure 2.3) is an important one, because, as I stated earlier, it is usually the time new sidesteps start to arrive in a particular category. Because performance improvement has slowed down, and most of the good customers have already adopted the new innovation, there are strong motivations for vendors to create a sidestep in order to increase the size of their markets.

To see this in living colour, we return again, for a moment, to the story of steam, and in particular to the reasons steam locomotion was killed off by two new technologies: internal combustion and the electric motor. Both these technologies were moved to railways at point D of our figure, sometime around 1920.

Steam innovation didn't cease immediately, though the pace of development slowed dramatically, and each new steam improvement made incrementally less difference. Inventions such as, for example, double-acting pistons (which admitted steam at the top and bottom of each stroke), effectively doubled the power of the engine. Then inventors started to use the waste steam from these strokes in smaller, less powerful subsidiary pistons to get even more work out of each unit of steam. Next, there was the realisation that waste steam, which was now at a relatively low pressure, could be re-condensed and returned to the boiler, rather than expelled.

All these incremental innovations, and many others, eventually led to the penultimate steam engine, the Mallard, which entered service in 1938 in the United Kingdom. It was capable of speeds in excess of 100 miles per hour (160 km/h), and holds the speed record for a steam engine.

Meanwhile, the first diesel engines had developed by 1892, but were no threat to steam, despite the fact they were extremely efficient. They were much better than steam in terms of raw horsepower delivered per unit of fuel, but what diesel *did* require was a whole new engineering infrastructure quite different from that already built around steam. The machines and people needed to operate diesel were simply not easily available to railroads of the time, so making them cost effective was impossible.

Around the same time, the first experiments were also beginning with electric railways. These too, were extremely efficient, once the problems of supplying power through a third rail were solved. Of course, very few railways could see much point in investing in such rails – or even more expensively, overhead wiring – since steam was continuing to be an effective and efficient substitute.

By 1917, inventors had worked out that neither diesel nor electric engines were all that satisfactory on their own, and had combined the two. The diesel engine was used to generate electricity, which then powered the traction motors that provided the motive force. This arrangement required only diesel fuel and was therefore superior to the steam engines then in widespread use, which also required a supply of water. It was also very efficient, required less maintenance and upkeep, and could be operated with very few men compared to steam.

When, in 1920, the first diesel-electric railway was opened, the die was cast for steam. It was simply more expensive to operate than the new engines, and diesel-electric began a period of explosive growth, just as steam had done when Stephenson demonstrated the economic viability of rail a century before. With each year that passed, steam became less attractive to operators, and by 1980, most countries had eliminated their steam infrastructures all together.

Diesel-electric is currently at its highest penetration level, but of course, it is also subject to sidesteps itself. The latest development is the pure electric, high-speed railway. This is a move sidestep that makes it possible for trains to replace airplanes on short haul routes.

What is the likely result? Over the next few decades, frustrated with the inconvenience of airports, anti-terrorism measures and the lack of city centre termini, passengers will migrate from air to rail transport. At least, for transcontinental journeys of a few hours or less.

TWO KINDS OF SIDESTEP

In Chapter 1, I defined a sidestep as the process of taking an existing product or service and tweaking it in some way that allows it to reach a bigger group of customers. With the discussions we've had thus far, we can now see how each of the two kinds of sidestep work in practice.

Dis/improve sidesteps enhance the price/performance ratio of any given product either by reducing the price or adding features (or both). This improvement results in a new value proposition for customers that makes the product attractive to segments which were previously disinterested. We can see this in Figure 2.4.

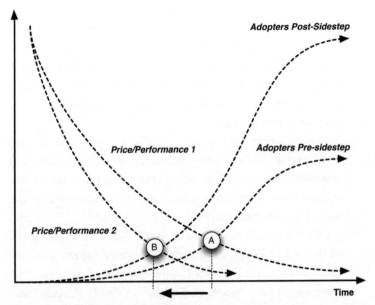

Figure 2.4 Dis/Improve Sidesteps

Assume the total price and performance of a particular product or service is represented by the curve at Price/Performance 1. On this curve, over time, the price and performance of the product or service improves until it reaches point A, which is the critical mass point for our S-curve that governs how information about the new idea is spreading. This is the point at which there are enough people who have heard about the product and where its economics make sense to a large group of them.

Now, whether you discount the price, or improve the features of the product (assuming you do so in a way that the over all price/performance is improved), it has the effect of shifting the curve to the left to Price/Performance No. 2.

In the case of airlines, for example, the dis/improve sidestep from economy class to a premium class increases the price, but also makes the product itself much better. If the improve sidestep is done right, the overall benefit improves at a greater rate than the price.

Ryan Air, the discount carrier we looked at earlier in this book, is a master of the dis/improve sidestep. The lack of free hold baggage, flight interconnect or frequent flyer rewards reduces the price of the product, but does it in such a way that the price reduction reduces over all benefits less rapidly than the decrease in performance.

This is obviously true for a discount carrier: you are still going to get from one place to another, probably quickly, and (hopefully) efficiently. The aircraft can still get into the air and transport you, no matter how uncomfortable and unpleasant the experience may be.

With a price/performance curve that's shifted to the left, as in the case of Price/Performance 2, a number of effects occur. Since more people can afford to use the product or service, the critical mass point moves to the left, to point B. Because more people use the service, there are more innovators, early adopters and other groups who are willing to try the product and service at the start. This is what drives the earlier and steeper S-curve.

Also, importantly, the improved price/performance results in a net increase in the total number of customers available. So, not only do things happen more quickly, the total market potential of the product is improved as well.

Whilst a dis/improve sidestep propels a product or service along its current trajectory by enhancing the price/performance so that more people are willing and able to buy, a move sidestep does something quite different, since it doesn't actually speed up the critical mass point.

You can see this in Figure 2.5.

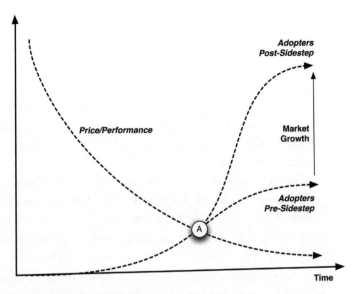

Figure 2.5: A Move Sidestep

We have already examined some examples of move sidesteps: Southwest Airlines, for example, shifted their product offer to serve travellers who would otherwise have used buses. Another was the use of steam power for locomotion, then latterly, the use of diesel-electric engines to replace steam.

All these sidesteps have one thing in common: they've taken a well understood product and moved it to a new market where it can be used to serve a new group of customers. The result is that the over all market for the product is grown, but with the advantage of there being substantial adoption in the previous one. In effect, the product reaches critical mass in two markets simultaneously. This accounts for the much steeper S-curve post-sidestep in Figure 2.5.

CONCLUSION

What we've uncovered in this chapter is, I think, interesting: you can execute a sidestep either by changing the price/performance of an existing product or service, or by moving an existing product or service to a new market which is similar enough to the old one that S-curve dynamics aren't forced to start from the beginning. Practically speaking, neither of these things is especially difficult to do.

The problem is when something is simple, the possible set of organisations who are capable of making a sidestep is large. The upshot of this is that whenever a sidestep is possible, it is likely there will be a large number of competitors who have already spotted the opportunity as well. Consequently, any place where there is an obvious chance to sidestep is usually pretty crowded. In crowded marketplaces, you get commoditisation, which leads, ultimately, to a race to provide the lowest price.

Providing the lowest price for a product is usually not a business strategy that leads to the kinds of returns that make modern businesses attractive to stakeholders. How then, in a world with easy sidesteps, do you protect prices and make reasonable returns? The answer is to incorporate a twist, the subject to which we'll turn in the next chapter.

KEEPING COMPETITORS OUT

··

CHAPTER THREE

I n most markets, it is a combination of supply and demand that results in a particular price. As we saw earlier, sidesteps are all about managing demand by manipulating price/performance and adoption S-curves.

Basic economics tells us that if demand expands, suppliers will enter markets to provide a service. When they do, prices drop as everyone strives to get as many customers as possible. Since a new, lower price favours later entrants (whose costs are lower because they haven't had to make all the first-mover mistakes), it is natural for those going into new business to try to stop anyone else following them.

What mechanisms do companies have to do this? Patents, trade secrets and copyrights are traditionally favoured ways of locking out organisations that might try to copy any great sidestep.

In Chapter 1, we saw how Fleming, the father of modern electronics, tried to use patent protections to control use of his oscillation valve. He probably thought doing so would give him a significantly better chance of getting rich. Surely, with a monopoly on his amazing new device, the market would be forced to beat a path to his door? Despite numerous legal battles, it was De Forest, whose copy-cat device was only slightly different to Fleming's, who made all the money when it was embedded in various desirable consumer electronic applications.

Fleming's problem was that he attempted to use the legal protection of a patent to make information about the oscillation valve scarce so he could charge for its use. Such scarcity is entirely artificial, especially considering a patent application requires full public disclosure. It doesn't take very much to change an invention enough that it can circumvent a patent, as Fleming found out to his cost.

In the past, scarcity was the basis of creating value. Patent protections, trade secrets, copyrights and other similar mechanisms are ways of doing this with ideas. Information may be intangible, but if you control who can access it, you're in a position to charge a price.

At an ultra-macro level, even physical goods and services are priced as a result of information scarcity. How many patents go into that lorry which moves goods from farm to market? What price does a broadcaster charge for advertising because it has to pay royalties on copyrighted content it uses to attract viewers? How much does Coca-Cola charge its bottlers for syrup whose ingredients are known only to a few senior executives?

Things are different now, though. Today's consumers are unaccustomed and unwilling to accept information scarcity. Digital goods and services are distributed with zero marginal costs, after all. Universally indexed data by services such as Google make it relatively easy to find ways to avoid patents.

Even trade secrets are routinely reverse engineered by groups of people with (sometimes) esoteric motivations for doing so. Consider, for example, one of the most famous trade secrets in the world: the syrup recipe for Coca-Cola. The syrup, which Coca-Cola bottlers purchase to mix into the actual drink under licence, is reputedly known to only a few executives in the company. So important does Coke value this information, they have, on at least two occasions, refused to reveal how they make the syrup, even in the face of court orders.

In 2001, a small open-source software company in

Canada decided to demonstrate how its methods for building programmes could bring about fundamental changes in the marketplace. To prove this, they set about replicating the super-secret recipe for Coke. Then they published their first attempt online. Each following iteration was also published online. Then each development of the recipe was taste-tested by huge numbers of people, who in turn offered suggestions for improvement and created new versions of the drink.

The result – OpenCola 1.0 – is pretty much indistinguishable from the real thing. The community of "recipe reverse engineers" quickly corrected such variations as showed up: OpenCola is now on version 1.13, and instructions for making it are published for all to see on the internet. So much for the inviolability of Coke's important recipe trade secret.

OpenCola – and too many other examples to list here – show that, in the modern world, traditional methods for protecting any competitive advantage founded on having a unique idea have become less effective every passing year. It is not too difficult to imagine the equilibrium price of information is tending towards zero, if it is not there already.

If one has an expectation that the price of an information resource will be nothing, competitive barriers which artificially move pricing upwards causes buyers to find alternatives. Of course, there are some goods and services where there is a natural demand, and in these cases, consumers almost always find ways to get around any competitive barriers deployed.

In 1998 a young hacker named Shawn Fanning created Napster, the first widely adopted music file-sharing site. It was immensely popular immediately, with devastating effects on the music industry. When Napster arrived on the scene, the music industry was based on the notion of the inviolability of revenues as a result of copyright restrictions: one of those competitive barriers that impose artificial constraints on customers in order to enable the vendor to set a price.

A copyright enables authors and publishers to restrict who can distribute their products: in order to make money, it is usual to charge a fee every time a copy is made, shown or lent. Such restrictions make sense for artists and publishers, but they most certainly don't for those who have paid for a right to enjoy music. This is what Napster was designed to get around.

Napster enabled individuals to share music with each other. Record companies may not have been happy when friends gave each other copies of albums they'd bought, but Napster scaled this up so *anyone* could give copies to anyone else. The site was essentially a centralised directory of content stored on its users' hard disks. You'd go to the site, ask for a song, and Napster's software would use it's directory to establish a connection for copying.

The copying itself occurred between the user asking for the song and anyone who had a copy stored on their disks. With technology, Napster made it possible to do at incredible scale what friends had already been doing for years – making copies of tracks they'd bought and sharing them around on cassette tape or writeable CDs.

It is an illegal act to copy music and share it under copyright law in most countries. Of course, whilst it was just individuals doing the copying record companies and artists had little choice but to look in the other direction. What were they going to do, anyway? Investigate the music collections of every music owner? Napster changed the game because it made it possible for people who didn't know each other to trade music. At its popularity peak, more than 28 million people were illegally trading using the service.

For a while, Napster got away with it. But when heavy-metal rock band Metallica discovered its latest single was available on Napster even before commercial release, they started to investigate. To their horror, Metallica discovered their entire back catalogue was freely downloadable without payment.

Confronted with this direct to challenge to their royalty income, the band took legal action against Napster in 2000. Other artists followed, supported by their record companies.

The artists and record companies eventually won their battle with Napster. After a fairly protracted and expensive court hearing, they obtained an order forcing Napster to remove any music that infringed copyright laws whenever they were notified of a breach. Of course, as Napster didn't control the files themselves (which were on end-users' hard disks), and managed only its index, it was unable to comply. In 2001, Napster stopped operating, declaring bankruptcy shortly after.

The record companies might have won the battle with Napster, but they hardly won the war. In 2000, worldwide sales of music were worth US\$38.6 billion. By 2008, sales were down to US\$27.5 billion, leading to mass lay-offs in the recording industry. Industry analysts seem to agree that this decline is unlikely to reverse, and file sharing sites are as pervasive as ever, extending themselves to movies, television shows and every other kind of digital content available.

The story of Napster shows us how ineffective creating artificial information scarcity has become as a means for generating value. For traditional record companies, the scramble to find a business model that actually works in this new reality is on-going. But it is interesting to consider how the story might have been different if the recording industry had had a little more foresight. What might they have done differently which could have preserved their fortunes in the face of illegal copying?

If they'd dared, they could have pursued a competitive advantage based on *consumption*, not scarcity. That such models can work in music is evident when one examines the rise of Dispatch, an indie band formed in Vermont, United States, during the 1990s. They had no recording contract, and consequently no radio play time. Instead, they spent most of their time touring as relative unknowns, hoping for the big break – the one every band aspiring to fame hopes for, but almost never comes.

Since the chance of being seen by a recording industry scout is more remote the further away from a major centre you are, it is extremely likely that Dispatch would have remained an unknown, if not for Napster. The band used Napster to distribute recordings of their work, making them free to everyone. By sacrificing any royalty potential, Dispatch was able to generate a huge word-of-mouth following. This led to increased demand for them to play live, and those performances were also recorded and shared on Napster.

By 2007, their fan base was so large the band were able to sell-out three consecutive nights at New York's Madison Square Garden for charity, becoming the first independent band ever to headline at that venue. That this occurred three years after the band had stopped creating new music together makes this feat more remarkable.

Dispatch is an example of what can happen when artificial information scarcity is eliminated. By giving away the actual product – music – for free, the band were able to generate a sustainable income for their main business: touring and live performance.

Giving things away in order to generate a revenue stream from something else is hardly a brand new strategy. In fact, if we revisit Figure 2.4 (see page 63) in the context of Dispatch, what's obvious is we've been examining an example of an excellent dis/ improve sidestep: Dispatch moved the price/performance curve so far to the left by virtue of their pricing that anyone with even the remotest interest in their music was able to access it.

But the real key to Dispatch's success was they applied a twist, one that enabled them to earn money from the one thing for which supply was constrained: their personal live performances.

TWISTS ARE PLATFORMS

When you think about it, Dispatch (in common with any recording artist in the post-Napster era) actually has two groups of customers: those who like to listen to recorded music, and another who like to participate in live performances. The more people in the listening group, the larger the performance-watching group becomes.

By moving the price/performance curve as far as possible to the left, Dispatch ensured the largest possible market would be interested in tickets to their live performances. This strategy was very successful: the band's final official performance drew a live audience of 110,000 people, and was documented in a feature film, *The Last Dispatch*. It was the largest independent music event in history then, and remains so today.

Twists work by setting up situations where two or more groups of customers get more value as either (or both) increase consumption. This is quite the opposite of traditional business models based on scarcity, which operate by restricting consumption in order to ensure that prices can be maintained.

Dispatch is a great example of such a twist. As listeners consumed more of their recorded music, the number of live shows increased as well. Each time there was a live show, Dispatch was able to make more recorded music by sharing each show on the internet. It was a virtuous circle which benefited both groups of customers and the band.

Examples of twists that work in this kind of way are everywhere. For another example at its most base, consider a typical heterosexual dating website. For the site to be successful, there needs to be a critical mass of both men and women from which each selects prospective dates.

For most dating websites, there are many more men in the system than women. If you don't believe me, try this on a dating site: do a search for all the men within about 100 miles of you, then the same search for all the women. Divide one into the other, and you'll likely find the ratio of men to women is something between 2:1 and 7:1. Since that's the case, men almost always go to sites with more women, perhaps because they feel they'll have to compete less aggressively if there is a bigger pool of available dates.

This brings us to the first of several key features of twists: there is very often one side of the market which drives demand for the other. Earlier, we discussed this same effect in the context of readers and advertisers for newspapers.

In the case of dating websites, having more women subscribers gets you more male subscribers. The effect is disproportionate, as you will have discovered if you did the search on a dating site. Academics don't use the word twist to describe the way dating sites and other examples like it work. They are more comfortable with the term "multisided market", the study of which has become something of a hot topic since mega-hit internet companies based on the principle have arisen: companies like Facebook and Google.

In a multisided market, vendors provide a *platform* – the set of rules and transactions that enable two or more groups of customers to meet – so they can create increasing value with consumption. That's what our hypothetical dating site really is: a platform that links a multisided market of male and female customer groups. For the purposes of this book, though, we'll continue to call platforms and multisided markets "twists" for simplicity, especially as I'll be extending the concept.

What are the key things to consider when building platforms on which twists work? Firstly, consider how the vendor structures the pricing, particularly with respect to any differential between the groups of customers that are being served.

Let us assume, for the purposes of argument, that on our hypothetical dating site, the female joining decision is primarily dependent on factors like functionality. For example, females may prefer to use sites with specific capabilities that enable them to preserve their privacy and anonymity. Let us also assume that men have little care for such features and base their joining decisions entirely on how many women they have to choose from. In this case, there is disproportionate influence on men to join if there are more women present, so it makes sense for the operator to aggressively increase female membership, perhaps with a zero or at least very much reduced price.

Men, on the other hand, can expect to pay most of the costs for the site. In platform parlance, the men are the "money side" because that's where most of the revenue is coming from. This is what Dispatch did by subsidising those customers who liked to listen to their recorded music so they could encourage more people to pay for live performances. Those customers who wanted to participate in the live performance were the money side for Dispatch, so giving away recordings to everyone else made sure the maximum number of seats were routinely sold.

In the world of dating away from the internet, you see exactly this same effect. Because men are the money side, nightclub owners aggressively target female customers with "ladies nights", where free or cheaper drinks are offered. Owners know if there are more women present, it will attract greater numbers of men, who can be charged full rate or even premium prices for drinks.

For a platform vendor – the nightclub owner in this case – this is a revenue-maximising arrangement. Not only do more high-paying men come through the door if you give women low or zero price drinks, the men will pay full price for those same women *and* themselves (once they've managed to meet up) because custom dictates they should.

It is extremely common for platform operators to choose to subsidise the part of their business that's disproportionately effective. This strategy enables them to steer customers on to their platform. This is especially important where there is a choice of platforms available to customers.

In almost every case where an easy sidestep is possible,

platform operators will face competition from other platforms. Invariably, the basis for such competition will be attracting the most important customers from the money side.

There are two important considerations here. The first occurs when both groups can choose any platform independently of each other. For example, if there are two nightclubs in town, and all other factors are equal, we might expect on a given night there will be a pretty even distribution of men and women in each. So, in this case, steering involves setting prices in such a way that the money side of the market – the men – are motivated to choose one club over the other.

The second point, which is much more interesting for the purposes of the twist, is the instance where one part of the market can choose multiple platforms, but the other can't. Let us continue with the nightclub metaphor for a moment and imagine one of the nightclubs offers not only free drinks to women, but has become the "go-to" place for ladies because the platform operator has secured the services of a special male revue on stage. Though they might choose from both nightclubs, most females are attending the one with the revue not only for the entertainment value, but probably because all their friends are going there, too.

This leaves the men in a difficult situation. They can go to the club with no females, but practically speaking will not do so. They are forced to attend the club with the revue – no matter how distasteful they might find it – simply because that's the only place they'll be able to find large numbers of women. They're forced into paying higher prices and watching a show that doesn't interest them.

The last question confronting any platform owner is the simplest: what is the plan for monetisation? There are two possible answers.

One is to charge by transaction. In transaction pricing, members on one or both sides pay a tariff based on how much usage they drive through the platform. In a nightclub, the transaction fee is any charge that's levied to get through the door, plus the per-drink costs that either side has to pay.

The other option is charging for membership. With membership pricing, one or both sides of the platform pay a fixed fee in order to access the platform on an on-going basis. Some nightclubs implement membership pricing (on top of their drink-based transaction pricing). The benefit of membership often includes guaranteed access even when the queues for entry are long, or, in some cases, access to a VIP area inside.

These three characteristics – subsidies, platform competition and a charging policy – define all possible permutations of the twist from a business model perspective. But just these three characteristics don't give us a complete picture yet: we still have to discuss the characteristics of the platform itself that make everything work. Let us turn our attention to that subject.

CONSUMPTION THAT IMPROVES THE PROPOSITION

Economists describe any process where increasing consumption improves the over all value for two groups in terms of "network externalities". Basically, the idea is there's some kind of value generated by consumption that's independent of any actual features of a product. This kind of thing is common knowledge to anyone who's taken the time to study how recent internet phenomena (such as social networking) operate.

Most modern analysis, however, focuses attention on just one aspect of the network effect: the case where the product becomes more useful as more people adopt it. Telephones, fax machines, computer networks and Facebook all exhibit this kind of network effect.

But there are other network effects that are somewhat less obvious, but just as powerful as drivers of value for platform operators. To see how these work, it is useful to return to the work of Everett Rogers, the innovation theorist who gave us our understanding of S-curves. By studying the spread of hundreds of ideas, Rogers realised there are five characteristics of innovations that govern the speed of the S-curve. Importantly for our discussion about twists, it works out you can create network effects on *any* of the five.

So, then: what are these five characteristics? For a summary, examine Table 3.1 below.

Innovation Attribute	Description	What Happens in a Twist
Observability	The innovation is easier to watch and copy in action than any previous alternative	Usage increases due to viral effects
Trialability	The innovation is easier to learn about than previous alternatives	Increasing number of trials result in "emergent behaviour"
Consistency	The innovation is more consistent with what a customer is used to than previous alternatives	Increasing usage results in herd behaviour
Relative Advantage	The product has a better functionality than any previous alternative	With increasing usage of the platform, functionality increases, driving cost/ performance ratio improvement
Complexity	The innovation is simpler to use than any previous alternative	With increase usage of the platform, complexity declines, driving a cost/performance ratio improvement

Table 3.1: Innovation Attributes and their Relationship to Twists

Observability

The first attribute is observability, which is any mechanism that permits a product to be seen in action. For example, if you have a friend who has a hot new gadget, and you get to look over his or her shoulder, you're experiencing observability. Practically speaking, in the real world the option to look over people's shoulders is limited to close friends and families. So products generally have to be specifically designed if they want to optimise the observability attribute.

When a product or service is observable, it moves the adoption S-curve to the left, speeding up the rate of adoption, because there's a very real difference between hearing about how something new works from a trusted party and actually witnessing it working with your own eyes.

I remember very clearly the first time I saw an automated check-in kiosk at an airport. They were easy to see because there were no queues waiting to use them. This was despite the fact that there were *monstrous* lines to deal with at the traditional check-in counters.

It is impossible that none of the people queuing knew about the check-in machines. After all, they were very visible, complete with helpful usage instructions written in big writing you couldn't possibly miss.

But airports are stressful places. If you're not checked-in on time, you're probably going to miss your flight and forfeit your fare. If you've never seen a check-in machine before, will you really take the risk that everything is going to go smoothly? And if it doesn't, aren't you going to have to queue anyway at the counter? Far better just to get in the queue you know will work in the first place.

The problem here is simple: kiosks of any kind just aren't that observable by others. If someone uses one, they're the only ones who can see what's going on because their bodies block the view. Queues were forming because no one had any observable evidence that check-in machines would work, so they didn't care to take the risk that something might go wrong.

The next time I flew, I noted the airline had begun using floor walkers to pull people out of the check-in queues. They'd then help travellers with automated check-in, making sure everything they did was fully observable by the customer and anyone the customer was travelling with. This strategy eventually worked. Now, every traveller I know has no problem at all with automated check-in.

What happens when you make observability a key part of a platform by rewarding customers for making use of your product? The answer is a twist based on "viral effects". Viral effects twists are powerful, because, essentially, they work to do all your marketing and customer recruitment for you. Since the total value your customers gain from the product is dependent on how many other people they get to use the product, this is a twist that can build scale quickly.

But there is another advantage and it is this: viral effects twists are very, very sticky. The greater the value a customer generates from a viral effects twist, the more difficult it is for them to switch to another product. Why? Much of the benefit they're getting is dependent on the fact they've recruited many people to the platform. If they were to change to something else, they'd have to start the recruitment effort all over again. Moreover, their recruitees are also likely to be getting value from the platform in proportion to the number of people they've recruited. Are they likely to switch just because you ask? Not really.

Later on, when we examine the viral effects twist in more detail, we'll see how companies such as Amway and Twitter have built defensible competitive advantage using this technique.

Trialability

The second innovation attribute is trialability. When people come across a new idea, the decision process, in the minds of customers, is mainly working out in advance whether something will be beneficial or not compared to what they're doing now. Making that determination from marketing materials and recommendations from others is difficult. Actually trying it themselves, though, is another thing altogether. Software marketing has been changed substantially by the realisation that trialability is a key determinant of purchase, especially in the consumer space.

In the past, most "real" software was sold in a box with traditional retail distribution. Customers were forced to find information sources they trusted in order to evaluate the likely risk of a particular purchase, so they turned to computer clubs, magazine reviews and their friends to find information to reduce the risk of the purchase decision.

Slightly later on, as floppy disks and CDs became cheaper, trial versions of software were made available free of charge. It was not uncommon, for example, for computer magazines to distribute a disk full of different titles for their readers every month. These methods have lately been replaced by the internet, which has the benefit of making trials completely free for the supplier. Since there is no economic downside to offering a trial in an age of digital distribution, everyone does it.

Trialability speeds up the S-curve because there is less risk a choice will work out badly for a potential customer once they've tried it for themselves. Consequently, they're much more willing to experiment.

Now, what happens when trialability is used in the context of a twist? Following the pattern of before, as consumption of an extremely trialable product increases, there should be a network effect so the over all value of the platform increases. When a platform increases in value because of the number of trials that have occurred, *emergent wisdom* develops from the crowd.

What is emergent wisdom? It develops any time large groups of people try things and there is a mechanism for them to aggregate their results; the outcome is often a powerful bottom-up understanding of the product or service being offered.

For example, there is much present interest in the concept of "prediction markets", which are examples of platforms that create emergent wisdom. Players bet real or play money on the likelihood of certain predictions coming true. When there are a large enough group of players, the prediction market can – to a degree – foretell the future.

Such markets have a long and colourful history. Formal betting markets using real money were common in US Presidential Election races until at least 1940. They were popular: there were thousands of participants, betting millions of dollars. And they were accurate: in only one case did the actual result differ from what the market predicted one month before voting day.

These days, much of the action has moved to the internet, where one of the most popular markets is the Hollywood Stock Exchange. On the site, players buy and sell shares in movies, actors, directors and other film-related options. It, too, has been a better than average predictor of the future: in 2006 it correctly predicted 32 of the 39 big category winners at the Oscars.

What is going on in a prediction market like the Hollywood Stock Exchange? The answer is that crowds of people contribute their individual experiences with movies, actors and directors (essentially, *trials* of the entertainment), and the betting mechanism aggregates the total to provide a very close indication of what the majority are thinking.

Of course, prediction markets aren't the only kind of emergent wisdom it is possible to get from a platform. Later on, we'll be looking at twists where self-experimentation leads to new medical discoveries, and the reasons why everyone automatically stands on the same side of an escalator whether or not they've been asked to do so.

Consistency with norms

The third innovation attribute described by Rogers is consistency with norms.

People don't like change much, because it forces them into new ways of thinking, and sometimes requires them to change deeply ingrained habits. This all requires effort, and it is human nature to minimise effort if at all possible. Consequently, any new product which requires new habits or new ways of thinking – those which are, in other words, inconsistent with whatever a customer experiences at the moment – take longer to adopt than otherwise.

Consider, for example, the introduction of automatic teller machines in banking. Now, you'd think the advantages of ATM machines would be enough to convince anyone they should use them routinely. Yet, despite the obvious advantages of cash on demand, there is a whole demographic for whom branch banking is the preferred, indeed the only, way to manage cash.

It is probably a generalisation to say this demographic is mainly older, but practically speaking, anyone who's spent many years going to branches to get their weekly supply of cash, has quite a bit to change if they want to make use of newer banking methods.

Instead of a single withdrawal once a week, they now need to get into the habit of going to a machine the moment they need cash. They have to remember their balance, because there is no longer any deposit book they can check. They also need to substitute their familiar signature with a hard-to-recall PIN number. When you add all this up, it's difficult for those in the habit of using branch banking to switch to using ATMs unless they've had the chance to view lots of other people making the switch successfully.

Some interesting effects start when you build a platform where increasing consumption *enhances* consistency with norms. Herd behaviours start to develop: customers do more of what they're doing because they see everyone else doing the same. Herd behaviours operate to make people in a group work together without any pre-planned direction. Stock market bubbles are an example: there's typically a period of frenzied buying (the bubble), followed by further periods of frenzied selling (the crash).

In the most interesting cases, this kind of thing can happen regardless of any underlying business fundamentals: it is the collective greed and irrationality of the "herd" which causes behaviour which appears irrational if you're looking in from the outside.

An example of a platform that uses herd behaviours to great effect is Amazon's recommendation engine, which though not unprecedented when it was introduced, is arguably what has driven much of the retail giant's success in the last decade. On Amazon, when you make a purchase decision, you're offered the opportunity to see what other items people bought who purchased that item as well. Moreover, Amazon will often offer you a discount price if you purchase the original item as well as the one it recommends. As the universe of total purchasers increases, the recommendation engine is better able to work out how to report herd behaviour, which in turn, increases purchase propensity.

These three attributes – trialability, observability and consistency with norms – have similar effects when implemented in a platform. They all speed up the S-curve, as shown in Figure 3.1.

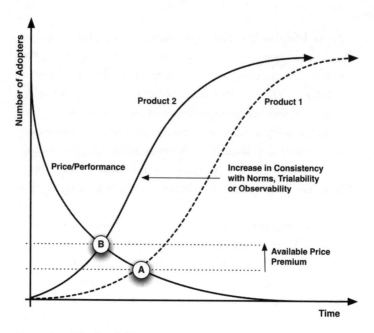

Figure 3.1: The Single Twist

Imagine an existing product is available which can service the customer's needs with the S-curve of Product 1. At point A, both the economics (represented by the price/performance curve) and knowledge about this product are at the point where critical mass can occur, and the product takes off.

Now, imagine further that a competitor introduces a new product (Product 2), but it is one that incorporates a twist, perhaps a platform that enhances trialability as more is used. Now, what happens? As the product is used more, advantages begin to accrue to the customer, and it becomes easier for each new customer to make the adoption decision. Consequently, the new product's S-curve moves to the left over time.

This has interesting effects. Firstly, Product 2 can get to critical mass much more quickly than Product 1. This is shown at point B. It follows this product will likely win in the market, because twists all exhibit lock-in effects: once a customer has begun to get value (which they have been a part of creating for themselves), they are highly unlikely to switch. Ergo, the platform with critical mass first will usually defeat all others.

Secondly, moving the S-curve to the left has the advantage of changing the point on the price/performance curve at which Product 2 makes sense economically for a critical mass of adopters to switch. Product 2 therefore has two additional advantages over Product 1: it is possible to charge a premium to customers, if desired, because the additional functionality delivered by the twist is not available elsewhere; and Product 2 needs relatively less investment (to develop it to a point where it becomes economic), because more customers are willing to try it sooner than Product 1.

All three innovation attributes we've examined thus far have exactly this effect: they shift the adoption S-curve to the left. Because only one of the curves in Figure 3.1 is moved, I call platforms based on these attributes a *single twist*. The other two innovation attributes – complexity and relative advantage – move *both* curves around.

CONSUMPTION THAT IMPROVES THE PRODUCT

When you move both the price/performance curve *and* the S-curve at the same time, you've built a platform that implements a *double twist*. A double twist is especially powerful because it has the effect of speeding up adoption and growing the market at the same time.

Till now, the innovation attributes we've looked at have had the effect of shifting the economics of an innovation along an existing price/performance curve. Making something more observable, for example, may make it simpler for me to make an adoption decision, but it doesn't really change the product much.

The next two attributes *do* have that effect though: they're both about changing the way a product performs, feature-wise, at particular price points, as well as changing the speed of the S-curve.

Firstly, let's examine "relative advantage", which is the notion that a product performs better at a particular price point than that which it supersedes. Consumers are always quick to evaluate potential relative advantage benefits for themselves, which largely boil down to their desire to "get a deal". They love it when they can do more stuff for less money, or do more stuff than anyone else for nearly the same money.

This is the reason everyone has a new phone every two years, or a new car every three or so. Perfectly working products seem much less desirable in the face of alternatives that offer (or at least are perceived to offer) superior relative advantage.

The final innovation attribute we have to look at is complexity. Complexity is the amount of new learning a person has to do before they can achieve any benefits from using the product. This is quite different from the consistency with norms attribute we looked at earlier. Consistency with norms suggests products which can be used in substantially the same way as those that have gone before will be adopted more quickly. Complexity, on the other hand, is a measure of how much difference there is in a product that must be learnt before it is useful. The more complex a product is, obviously, the slower adoption will be.

Now, in the context of a twist, what interests us is the case where increasing use of the product *reduces* the over all complexity for everyone. In other words, crowds of people, learning and sharing together, make it less difficult for other people to join their crowd.

Take, for example, various on-going attempts to capture all the world's knowledge in an encyclopaedic form. The traditional approach to this problem has always been to empanel a group of experts who, together, write the information into a series of articles, usually published in many book volumes.

This approach, unfortunately, suffers from a couple of problems. Firstly, the total number of articles is small in comparison to everything known, and therefore, the chance of finding information on any subject even the least bit unusual or specialist is remote. Even worse, though, is the problem of timeliness: articles are often out of date almost as soon as they're written. The root of the problem is the amount of work you can get out of a small editorial team is finite, but the world's knowledge grows in exponential fashion each day.

Wikipedia, the internet encyclopaedia, solves this problem by implementing a twist based on reduction of complexity with consumption. With Wikipedia, every reader can *also* be an author. Most people choose only to read articles but at least one third contribute on a regular or semi-regular basis. What is interesting about those who contribute to Wikipedia – they call themselves Wikipedians – is their motivation for spending their time making the encyclopaedia better.

In a global survey[5] of self-selected Wikipedians, 72% reported their motivation as, "I like the idea of sharing knowledge and want to contribute to it", and 68% also said, "I saw an error I wanted to fix". No more than 2% were involved in updating the site for personal gain.

What is actually occurring in Wikipedia is a very large and complicated problem – codifying the world's knowledge – is divided into manageable units as Wikipedia is used and expanded. With one in three new users expanding and updating the site, the traditional encyclopaedia has little chance to compete either in breadth or timeliness. Unsurprisingly, this has had the effect of all but eliminating the business of traditional publications like *Encyclopaedia Britannica*.

---

5   Global Wikipedia Survey 2010, Collaborative Creativity Group, United Nations University.

Let us now look at how reducing complexity or increasing relative advantage works theoretically, by referring to Figure 3.2.

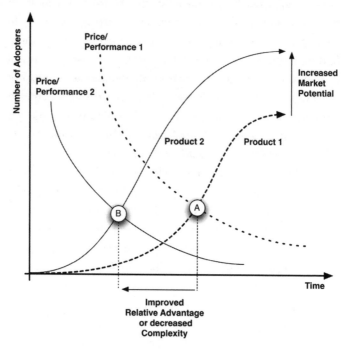

Figure 3.2: The Double Twist

We start by examining the S-curve for Product 1. The product is probably one that's the result of a traditional sidestep, and has been improving in price/performance to point A, where it has achieved critical mass. The economics at this point are sufficiently good that enough people can afford the product and, additionally, a large enough body of people have awareness of it that critical mass is possible. In the meantime, a new product, Product 2, is released which incorporates a twist based on increasing relative advantage or reduction in complexity. This has a surprising and powerful effect.

Firstly, reduction in complexity or increasing relative

advantage doesn't just move the needle on an *existing* price/performance curve, because the actual features of the product are being modified by the platform itself. The result is that a *completely new* price/performance curve is achieved, which is shown as Price/Performance 2.

The change in the price/performance curve has the effect of making a *much* larger group of customers available to try the product, so the total market is grown in much the same way as in the case of a sidestep alone. Consider the case of Wikipedia, for example: if one of every three new users is adding more articles, the *total* number of new readers the encyclopedia can address grows, because the chance a brand new information seeker will find what he or she wants in Wikipedia becomes greater with the number of articles.

So the change in the price/performance curve is half the double twist, and the other part is the acceleration of the S-curve itself. Remember that decreasing complexity or increasing relative advantage both have the effect of shifting the S-curve to the left, speeding up over all adoption. When this happens, the new equilibrium for Product 2 shifts to point B, which is *much* earlier than for Product 1.

In any competitive situation, therefore, where Product 1 (without a twist), competes with Product 2 (with a double twist), the latter will certainly win. Not only does it have a much larger addressable market – one which grows as more consumers adopt – but it can get to the point where most consumers will adopt by default much more quickly.

With our understanding of the underlying mechanics of twists complete, let us now turn to one of the best examples where the sidestep and twist has created one of the most successful companies ever: Microsoft Corporation.

HOW MICROSOFT WON THE SOFTWARE WAR

Microsoft has been a major force in computing for the last three decades. People either love or hate it. It is one of those semi-religious issues one regularly encounters wherever passionate people are involved in something they care about. The central issue of such a debate is often whether Microsoft has achieved its success as a result of innovative behaviour in its own right, or because it has been good at following where others have led the way.

Microsoft *is* an innovative company. Any organisation investing billions every year in research and development cannot fail to create original products and services. But Microsoft's genuine technological breakthroughs, like those of everyone else, are almost never commercially successful. Spectacular as they may be, they hardly ever win over the hearts and minds of consumers and enterprises. When Microsoft *has* been successful, it has taken technology that's previously proved valuable elsewhere, technology with existing demand, and applied various single and double twists to lock out competitors.

Year	Sidestep	Twist	Revenue
1978	Microsoft moves high level programming languages from shared to personal computers	Double twist: increasing relative advantage as more programmers write for BASIC	US$1 million
1983	Microsoft duplicates CP/M and moves it to the IBM PC	Double twist: increasing relative advantage as developers build more software for PC	US$18 million

1987	Microsoft copies the user interface of Macintosh and brings it to the PC	Single twist: packaging Windows with Word and Excel expands usage of Windows with consumption of productivity apps	US$345 million
1997	Copy NCSA Mosaic and embed in browser in the operating system	Double Twist: increasing relative advantage as web sites begin to use Microsoft specific enhancements	US$11.36 billion

Table 3.2: Sidesteps and Twists at Microsoft

This, of course, is the very definition of the sidestep and twist strategy, so it is interesting to examine the company's history in a little bit of detail given what we have learned so far.

The story starts in 1975, when Bill Gates saw the January issue of *Popular Electronics*, then a popular magazine with technical hobbyists. Its pages described something quite new: a personal microcomputer cheap enough to be bought for use at home. This device, the Altair 8800, launched at just the right time. For at least 10 years before its release, young science and engineering graduates had been taught computer programming, a regularly required course of study. But most of these graduates, once they'd finished at school, had no access to a computer. From the moment the Altair was announced, it was a hit. Orders backed up for months.

By the standards of today, the first Altair was extraordinarily rudimentary. You "programmed" it by setting switches to represent binary codes, and the only way to tell what was going on inside the machine was watching a set of flashing lights on the front panel. Clearly, you'd have to be very geeky indeed to take much pleasure in doing that.

It didn't take the community of Altair owners long to rectify these shortcomings themselves. Using parts scrounged from other machines, they added paper tape storage and typewriter printers, enabling them to create programmes that could deal with words and letters, rather than flashing lights. It wasn't long before all these hobbyists began sharing their best paper tapes with each other.

Bill Gates and his friend Paul Allen saw an opportunity to sidestep. They believed they could move a more user-friendly programming system which used English language words to the Altair. Such systems were common on the large computers commonly used in business and at universities at the time. It was possible, they reasoned, that if they achieved this, they'd have a paper tape useful enough to be sold.

Gates and Allen got started immediately, although they had no computer on which to work. Instead, they "borrowed" time on the big and expensive computer at Harvard University, where Gates was studying at the time.

Eight weeks later, the duo had a tape that worked, and they rushed to demonstrate it to Altair[6]. So impressed were executives, the pair were offered a contract to bundle their work with every memory expansion card sold by Altair. For each copy, they were to receive between US$30 and US$60.

Problems were not far away though, because the memory boards Altair provided were slap-dash things, notoriously unreliable. Altair's customers – all extremely technical with advanced degrees in science and the like – responded by creating their own memory boards that actually worked. From that point onward, most Altair computers were purchased without a memory board, and therefore without Gates' computer language. Instead, hobbyists continued their practice of sharing tapes around.

---

6   The actual name of the company that produced the Altair was Micro Instrumentation and Telementary services and is simply named Altair from now on for ease of reading.

This infuriated Gates, who by this time had left his studies at Harvard to pursue his software business. Here, we can see the first nascent example of the double twist upon which Microsoft would later build an empire. Their computer language tape was a platform uniting two groups of Altair's customers: those who wished to make use of software, and those who wanted to provide it to the Altair community. Moreover, it created an ecosystem of related products – every programme written using the computer language made the language *itself* more valuable.

But for Microsoft, this first incarnation of their double twist faced a huge problem: there was no money side. Neither customer group were at all used to the idea of paying for software, especially when making copies was the simplest way to obtain it anyway. Setting a tone for which he would later become famous, Gates wrote an open letter to the Altair community – published in popular hobbyists magazines – accusing his prospective customers of stealing both his software and his lunch.

If nothing else, this initial experience working with twists taught the pair something valuable: twists without a money side aren't really all that useful as a business strategy. They tend to cause immediate discounting of the value of the platform – to a price of zero. Microsoft had to find a way to ensure it was part of the money side, and it quickly found an answer: embed its computer language in microchips that were part of the computer itself. Apart from anything else, this made the software impossible, or at the very least very difficult, to copy. The company signed deals with nearly everyone producing personal computers for home use in the market at the time. *This* twist was much more successful, because Microsoft's software was no longer an optional purchase and was directly embedded in the money side of the home computer business. Microsoft had taken its first baby steps to domination of the software market, and its revenues began to expand quickly. By the end of 1978, the company was earning US$1 million a year.

Microsoft's next sidestep and twist came a few years later, when computer giant IBM launched its own personal computer, cleverly named the "PC". It was 1981. IBM had noticed home computers were finding use in business contexts, and recognised it was way out of position if this was a trend that continued. They decided to rush a computer to market just in case, using off-the-shelf parts. Halfway through their development process, IBM worked out it needed software to make the computer actually work, and started looking around for a company that could provide it quickly.

When their approach to the market leaders at the time failed, IBM came to Microsoft. Gates and Allen had nothing to offer IBM when discussions opened: they were too busy selling copies of computer languages to hardware manufacturers and didn't then own the kind of software IBM was looking for.

However, just as they'd previously managed with Altair, the lack of an asset to sell didn't deter them. This time, however, the pair had no need to rely on their own efforts to create a product. Sales of computer languages had given them enough capital to buy a just-made control programme from a local programmer in Seattle. For Microsoft, this was another move sidestep.

Even at this early age, Gates was a canny – and even more importantly, visionary – businessman. He'd already guessed the potential for IBM's PC, and knew that a successful partnership would have significant benefits for Microsoft. Consequently, he gave IBM everything it asked for when the parties sat down to negotiate how the PC could be bundled with his control programme.

IBM failed to ask for one thing, though: *exclusivity*. Gates retained the right to sell his software to anyone who wanted it. When IBM's personal computer product hit the market, it was immediately successful. As the market for personal computers expanded, clever entrepreneurs everywhere spotted their own opportunity to sidestep into the market space IBM was creating.

Since IBM had used off-the-shelf parts for its PC, anyone

could easily duplicate its design. More importantly, though, Gates made it known he was willing to sell his control programme – now named MS-DOS – to anyone who wanted it. Apparently, this infuriated IBM, but it had the effect of creating huge adoption for the PC as a platform. There were more PCs than anything else, and it wasn't long before the PC architecture was the only viable one for business.

Once again, Microsoft had built a double twist. In this case, users demanded computers that ran MS-DOS because most interesting business programmes of the time were coming out on the PC platform first. All these programmes created an ecosystem of value that no end-user could afford to ignore.

Simultaneously, developers wanted to write for MS-DOS because IBM's PC architecture – with the burgeoning secondary market for "clones" made by third parties – was the most extensively deployed. Consequently, they had the biggest market of users who might buy their software.

By contrast with Microsoft's earlier forays into home computers, this time there was a money side independent of the hardware itself. Business users, unlike hobbyists, were willing to pay for programmes, and were therefore also willing to pay for the MS-DOS platform on which they would run.

It did not take long for Microsoft to eliminate all competing platforms in the business software market as a result of the network effects associated with the rise of IBM's PC and clones based on the same hardware. By the end of 1983, Microsoft achieved revenues of US$18 million a year, and the company expanded to 128 employees. Though it had seen off all competitors for the current generation of personal computers, Microsoft was about to face its next great battle.

A sidestep of a breakthrough technology into the personal computer market – graphical user interfaces – threatened to disrupt the comfortable position Microsoft had created for itself. The graphical user interface, or GUI, had been popularised by the release of two Apple products. The first of these was Lisa, available to the market in 1981, and loosely based on breakthrough innovations from Xerox.

Featuring a graphical user interface and mouse pointer, Lisa was ground-breaking, but commercially unsuccessful: its new features were not sufficiently compelling to offset its high price compared to the dominant PC from IBM.

Apple sold relatively few of the machines, and eventually dumped its whole inventory into a guarded landfill site in order to secure a significant tax write-off for what remained. The second release from Apple was Macintosh in 1984, a computer that also had a mouse, graphics displays featuring windows, and the ability to display information on screen in the same way as it would look on paper.

It was *much* more successful than its predecessor Lisa, mainly because Apple had finally found a way to get the price/performance ratio to a point where a significant number of users could actually make a reasonable case for trying it. In other words, it was much cheaper, and adoption began to expand.

Macintosh was a direct threat to Microsoft's control of personal computing. Microsoft signalled its intention to enter the space with its announcement of Windows that year, which it finally delivered in 1985. Little more than an add-on for MS-DOS, Windows 1.0 was hardly a huge success. It was much inferior to Macintosh. It had a mouse, but also needed to support keyboard commands because most PC users were yet to acquire the pointing device that came standard with the Mac.

There were few important programmes that ran on Windows, and adoption was slow. Users may have been willing to buy MS-DOS, but what was the point of a windowing system with so few products that actually used it?

Microsoft was, by now, the most experienced company software in the world at using twists based on ecosystems of complimentary products. It was very aware it had to get adoption of Windows up quickly. The business strategy was simple: it made the next version of its best-selling word processor and spread-sheet dependent on Windows 2.0, and included Windows free of charge on the same disk. Via this mechanism, Windows was automatically installed on the machines of every user of Excel and Word.

Through the device of steering users to Windows by subsidising its adoption so heavily, Microsoft eventually acquired its critical mass for Windows. The company still hadn't made much money from the product, but it was building a platform that would later become unassailable, even in the face of technically superior competitors, such as Macintosh.

When Microsoft released Windows 3.0 in 1990, the major revision was an instant hit. More than four million copies were distributed in the first year of sales, and almost 1200 new applications were written that year alone. Because Microsoft had the largest group of customers, developers were seriously considering whether there was any point writing software for any other operating system at all.

Windows 3.0 was finally a technically serious competitor to the previously superior Macintosh, because PC computers were finally being deployed with decent graphics capabilities and a mouse. Now that it had most of the users and most of the developers Microsoft had no further need to subsidise the money side of its platform and began to generate seriously windfall profits.

1990 was the first year that Microsoft broke US$1 billion in sales. With 5,635 employees, the company was now the largest software maker by far, and still, it continued its meteoric rise.

Whilst Microsoft was busy cementing its dominance in the new field of graphical user interfaces, another new trend had begun to be felt. The internet, initially the preserve of boffins in government and academia, had begun to spread to larger corporations, and even end users. The possibilities of a worldwide network began to catch the imagination of visionaries and inventors. In 1994, the world changed when the first rudimentary tools for browsing the World Wide Web appeared.

The best programme for the internet in 1994 was NCSA Mosaic, a web browser developed by the National Centre for Supercomputing in the United States. It was freely available for the majority of computing platforms then in common use, and its use of attractive graphics and other multimedia made it interesting for those jumping onto the internet bandwagon.

In October that year, *Wired Magazine*, in an article on the internet trend that appeared to be emerging, made a particularly prophetic remark when it suggested that Mosaic was "well on the way to becoming the world's standard interface" [7].

This was the first of many wake up calls for Microsoft, who by now were convinced their initial bet on graphical user interfaces was the correct one. They had by then released Windows 3.1, which was even more successful than the previous version. Whilst the actual experience of Windows was still inferior to that offered by Macintosh, there was no question that in the adoption stakes, Microsoft had won. Windows was the *de facto* standard for most people.

Perhaps it was because its attention was elsewhere, it seemed Microsoft didn't really notice the internet until an upstart company, called Netscape, released a new and improved browser that captured more than 80% of the market in a few months. By 1995, Netscape was the darling of the technology press, was listed on the Nasdaq, and was leading the charge into the coming dot-com boom.

For Microsoft, Netscape represented the biggest threat yet to its domination of personal computing. If the internet was the next great computer paradigm, then Netscape was already the window most people were using to access it. Windows had every chance of becoming irrelevant. Web browsers are platforms that

---

7   Wolfe, Gary. "The (Second Phase of the) Revolution Has Begun", *Wired Magazine* (October 1994).

implement a variation on the same double twist that Windows had used to dominate personal computing. The variation was web browsers united content consumers with content publishers rather than application developers with users.

But visionaries across the industry were predicting that, soon, there would be no difference between the two categories. People began to speak of a "universal client": one window which would unite them all.

For Microsoft, here was a fundamental threat: what if all the developers moved away from building Windows applications and started developing for the web instead? Moreover, if Navigator truly became the one access point everyone needed, what use was Windows?

Strategically, Microsoft had little choice but to build a browser of its own. When Microsoft eventually released a browser, it was significantly inferior to Navigator in almost every respect. Internet Explorer had fewer features and was quite a bit less stable than the Netscape product. And, because most people already *had* Navigator, there was no incentive at all for them to change, particularly given the fact that internet connections were still relatively expensive, and Explorer was a big, and time-consuming, external download.

Microsoft didn't have critical mass, and was unlikely to get it. Drastic measures were called for. First, it decided to make Internet Explorer free, hoping that by subsidising users it would catch up. However, and despite substantial investment to achieve feature parity, there was still little motivation for users to switch. Everyone was talking about Netscape, and that is where users stayed.

By 1996, Netscape had 85% of all internet users, and the danger to Windows was even more apparent as applications and content continued to merge. Microsoft had to do something. They responded by falling back on their tried and true strategy for getting a new product to critical mass: attach a product which already had significant demand to one that didn't. As they had previously done by bundling Windows 2.0 with Word and Excel, Microsoft now coupled Internet Explorer with Windows 98, and they combined the two so closely that Windows could no longer work without it.

That this was an obvious move to eliminate a competitive rival was not lost on Netscape *or* the regulators, who immediately went up in flames. By the end of 1998, Microsoft was in anti-trust proceedings with the United States Government, which later found it had abused its Windows monopoly to unfairly dominate the market and eliminate competition.

In the meantime, the launch party for Internet Explorer version 4, the first coupled deeply with Windows in this way, was said to be massive. Held in San Francisco, the party featured a huge "E" logo – the icon of Internet Explorer. Afterwards, the Internet Explorer engineering team stole it, apparently leaving it on the front lawn of Netscape's corporate headquarters the next day. Affixed to the massive Microsoft "E" was a note which cheekily said: "From the IE Team… we love you!"

Netscape's engineers were not delighted with this behaviour, and responded in kind the moment they arrived at work. Firstly, they kicked over the Microsoft "E", and erected their own dinosaur logo on top. Then, they affixed a sign reading: "Netscape 72, Microsoft 12", which was the reported market share of the two browsers at the time. Netscape's happy market position did not, however, last. By the end of 1998, Internet Explorer's market share had doubled. The next year it doubled again, and by the turn of the millennium, Microsoft had almost 85% of the market.

Netscape, unable to keep up the fight, also made its browser freely available, and was eventually acquired by online services provider AOL. By 2002, Microsoft held more than 90% market share in the browser space, representing the peak of its penetration, and Netscape was no longer a significant market player.

So far, we've seen how Microsoft took ownership of three paradigm shifts in computing using a sidestep and twist strategy.

Firstly, it dominated the emerging market of home computers by sidestepping a computer language from mainframes to the new machines, and getting more developers than anyone else by virtue of bundling with the machines themselves. Then, it sidestepped an operating system it bought from a local author into the IBM PC, and made sure it had more users than anyone else by practically giving it away with every personal computer sold, no matter the manufacturer. Next, it sidestepped the Macintosh user interface to MS-DOS and created Windows, driving it to critical mass on the back of Word and Excel. Finally, it sidestepped a web browser into Windows, ensuring its browser was most widely adopted by tightly coupling it to the operating system that 90% of all users had already.

In all four cases, sidesteps were taken down the price/performance curve artificially through the use of bundling strategies which drove adoption to critical mass. Surely, with such successes under its belt, Microsoft could rightly have assumed that all subsequent threats could be routinely handled in the same way.

However, the company's later history has not been so successful. The most recent paradigm shift – presently under way – is from personal computers to various mobile devices such as smartphones and tablet computers. For once, Microsoft has found itself out of place in this new digital market. The reason? It failed to implement an effective sidestep and twist in the face of determined competition from Apple and Google.

By contrast, both those companies have employed such a strategy successfully. It is a story we will examine in a little bit more detail further on.

SUMMARY

There are three main points we've discussed in this chapter.

The first concerned the essence of a twist, which can be defined as creating competitive advantage with increasing consumption rather than constraining supply. When companies build products that get better as they're used, they tend to win, particularly when they do things to ensure they get to a critical mass of users quickly.

The second point was that twists work when there are two or more groups of customers who each get value from the other as consumption expands. As we've just seen in our examination of Microsoft's sidesteps and twists, it has always won when it has managed to create a virtuous circle of demand between developers and end users on its various system platforms.

The final point is this: twists are based on the idea that the five defining attributes of innovations can all be arranged in such a way that they create network effects. Relative advantage and complexity, for example, when turned into a twist, cause the actual product to improve as it is used. This is a topic we'll explore in more detail in Chapter 5.

On the other hand, trialability, consistency and observability are attributes which, when used as part of a twist, improve those parts of a proposition not directly part of the product with consumption. It is this latter case, the single twist, which we'll explore in more detail in the next chapter.

THE
SINGLE TWIST

CHAPTER
FOUR

n 1930, a medical doctor named Carl Rehnborg returned to the United States after spending a decade in China. During his visit, he'd been exposed to some of the worst examples of malnutrition he'd ever seen. In some cases, he also saw some seemingly miraculous cures. These, he realised, were the result of China's superior understanding of the roles of vitamins and nutrients in health.

Inspired, Dr. Rehnborg returned to the United States, where he invented the first mass-produced multi-vitamin for general consumption. At this particular time, vitamins were an unknown product category. Neither a medicine nor a food, they weren't carried at supermarkets or pharmacies. And since almost all consumers were unfamiliar with the basics of nutrition, *selling* vitamins proved as difficult as creating them in the first place. So Dr. Rehnborg did what any struggling entrepreneur would have done: he set up his own company, and went on the road himself to build his business. He named his business Nutrilite.

Success came slowly, mainly because any improvements in health derived from supplements were extremely gradual. It took time for customers to see any results, but Dr. Rehnborg persisted. Eventually, Nutrilite's customers began to see their health improve, and started telling their friends about the "miracle pills" the company was producing. Since you couldn't get the pills in shops, Nutrilite's early customers began distributing the product to their friends in exchange for a discount on their own supplements.

It wasn't long before customers were distributing to other customers, who were actually buying the product. And, over time, the number of links in the chain continued to expand. The multilayer distribution model took off. Dr Rehnborg and Nutrilite had just invented a new way of doing business: multilevel marketing.

It was a simple idea: every person in the system had *two* income streams. The first was the profit you made when you sold the product directly. The second, potentially much greater income stream, was derived from a royalty you received every time someone you'd recruited made a profit. Nutrilite continued to expand using this innovative business model.

Eventually, in 1949, Nutrilite came to the attention of two school friends, Jay Van Andel and Richard DeVos. The pair quickly managed to sign up a network of over 5,000 people with a simple pitch: "Your personal returns will be based on how many other people you recruit like you. And if you want proof, just look at us, we're rich!"

What they had done was implement a classic invocation of a twist: they built a platform where the over all value increased as consumption expanded. In their case, the twist was based on the observability innovation attribute we examined in Chapter 3.

This is where the story gets interesting. As their profits and influence grew, Van Andel and DeVos realised they were too dependent on the fortunes of Nutrilite. Any interruption to the supply of the product would have decimated their incomes.

When, a few years later, Nutrilite ran into issues with various government regulators, it was the straw that broke the camel's back. The pair swiftly formed a business association with their top distributors, and bought the exclusive rights to manufacture and sell cleaning fluids for the home. The business association was called The American Way Corporation, and later became known simply as Amway. Amway went on to huge success, becoming so large it was able to acquire a majority stake in Nutrilite in 1974, and become outright owners 20 years later.

What does the story of Amway tell us about the sidestep and twist? If there is one lesson we can learn, it is this: though Van Andel and Devos started their network on the back of vitamin sales, it was relatively simple for the pair to switch to another product category when it made sense to do so. It was simple because the pair controlled a platform, one that united buyers and sellers of domestic products. The product itself was less important than the fact that sellers saw increasing returns from consumption of the multilevel marketing programme.

VIRAL EFFECTS TWIST

Multilevel marketing is an example of a single twist based on increasing returns from observability. It is an instance of a business model which is more widely known as a "viral business" – a business which grows because there is some implicit motivation by platform users to expand usage. Viral businesses and viral products are the result of one of two psychological dynamics. One of the reasons people want to share is because they achieve some kind of personal gain from doing so. The other is because they get to feel good when they share.

In order to build a viral effects twist, then, one needs to construct a platform in which one (or both) of these dynamics increase with consumption. At Amway, the motivation for sharing is purely selfish – distributors are motivated to recruit other distributors to help them make sales, since this increases their personal income.

Let us examine a much more recent case of this kind of twist: the short message service Twitter. Twitter is, itself, the product of a sidestep. Initially, the service was conceptualised as a way to send status updates to many people from a cell phone. It was an incremental idea based on something that was already extremely widely adopted: short message services offered by telecommunications companies.

SMS adoption is highest amongst teenagers and young adults. Twitter, however, is used mainly by older adults, particularly those who have not used any other social network before Twitter. In fact, only 11% of Twitter's users are aged between 12 and 17[8.] The move sidestep of Twitter has, therefore, achieved a significant increase in *over all* usage of various short messaging services.

What do all these users do with the service? The answer is interesting.

According to an analysis by research firm Pear Analytics, 40% is pointless babble. "I just had lunch", and "On the way home" and other such tweets fall into this category. The rest of the traffic is random conversations between people, broadcasts of things people feel interesting enough to share, and a not insignificant percentage of the remainder is gratuitous self-promotion.

The most interesting thing about Twitter is that at least 34% of users have never issued a single tweet. And most tweets originate from just a quarter of the users of the service.

What does this tell us? Two things: firstly most people are tweet consumers, if they are monitoring the service at all. Secondly, if most people are tweet consumers, there must be some kind of value that accrues to tweet producers to motivate them to tweet in the first place. It is hard to ignore the possibility there is an inherent value in being a Twitter user with a large number of followers, and therefore that people are actively recruiting. This is an intuitive result when you consider the way the "selfish" viral effects twist works.

---

8   ComScore data.

Interestingly, the way people behave on Twitter in recruitment of followers is, in many ways, similar to the way distributors behave at Amway; but unlike the case of Twitter, we have some interesting financial statistics we can use to estimate the way the selfish viral effect twist works.

Most Amway distributors earned about US$115 per month in 2005, according to data in the company's compensation plan documents. Just over 0.16% of distributors made US$3,956 per month if they were close to the top of the Amway pyramid. For those actually at the top, only 0.01% of distributors, the revenue per month was US$12,249[9]. As you can see, most of the value accrues to those at the top of the pyramid. This is true for most viral effects twists which have selfishness as the underlying behavioural dynamic.

The other kind of viral effects twists are those based on altruistic motivations. Users spread the benefits of platform usage because it benefits others, rather than themselves. One of the most interesting stories of a viral twist based on altruism is that of microfinance – the practice of making small loans to prospective entrepreneurs in the developing world so they can start businesses which make them self sufficient and lift them out of poverty. Now, as you'd imagine, these are people at the very bottom of the financial food chain. They have no assets, and very often, no regular income either. They are certainly not the kinds of customers that traditional banks are interested in.

Anyway, in 1974, a hideous famine struck the people of Bangladesh. With crops failing and the government too poor to support them economically, the harshest kind of poverty befell the struggling masses. Some estimates put the total death toll at greater than 1.5 million people, with by far the greatest percentage of deaths amongst "wage workers": those without land of their own.

For a few, very few lucky souls, help was at hand. An

9   Data reported on Wikipedia, accessed June 2011

unknown economics professor, Muhammad Yanus, decided to try an unusual experiment: start a bank which lent money to people based not on their ability to repay, but on the value of the borrower as a person as determined by his or her peers. Professor Yanus lent US$1 to 42 impoverished bamboo stool makers for raw materials. The loans led to a breakthrough discovery: those at the bottom of the financial food chain not only repaid loans, they did so with interest and very rapidly. All 42 of the craftsmen to whom Yanus lent money pulled themselves out of poverty and created viable incomes for themselves and their families.

Professor Yanus used his knowledge to found the world's first microfinance bank – Grameen Rural Bank – on the principal that lending decisions should henceforth be made on the basis of the potential of a person, not their ability to repay. He won the Nobel Peace Prize in 2006 for his achievement, in recognition for helping thousands out of poverty by making it possible for the poor to help themselves.

It was in 2003 that Professor Yanus paid a visit to Stamford Business School, where he gave a lecture on microfinance. In the audience were Jessica Jackley and her husband Matt Flannery. For both, this lecture was a call to action. By 2005, they'd launched a website where people in the developed world could send money to developing-world entrepreneurs.

On the site, Kiva.org, anyone needing support could post their business ideas, and those with money to lend were able to indicate which people they'd like to invest in. Now, here is the interesting thing about Kiva: lenders do not receive any interest payments, though they get their principal back in time if the loan is repaid.

By June, 2011, Kiva had written loans worth US$216 million, and there were almost 600,000 people registered who were helping fund them. The average amount invested in loans by the average Kiva user is US$232.24, and of that, only about US$2.05 is not repaid.

Now, what are the features of the Kiva platform that have enabled this altruistic viral effects twist to work? Firstly, lenders are able to join communities of like-minded people who all share the same reasons for being on Kiva. Self-organising into teams, these communities connect with each other in order to rally around lending goals they all believe in. Friends and family often join the same communities, because the joy of giving is better shared.

There are other features in Kiva that drive the viral effects twist, though. For altruism to be driving viral behaviour, there has to be something users want to share. In Kiva, this is done by telling stories about borrowers and the use to which they've put their money when they're granted a loan.

Here is an example I randomly selected from the Kiva site: "Lukwago Aisha is the leader of her lending group in Jinja, Uganda. She is 35 years old, and married with four children, takes care of her parents, and looks after three orphans. She is a tailor and also sells cloth materials. Her major challenge is the limited capital she has, so often does not have stock to sell."

One hundred and fifty-eight individuals from the developed world signed up to help Aisha and her group build their business. Most were individuals, but nearly 20% of the money came from lending communities. Each lender has their photo associated with loan, and the total portfolio of loans for each lender is also publicly available. Want to get people to join Kiva? All you have to do is show them your portfolio to get a collection of inspiring stories about the good you have personally helped achieve in the developing world.

What do Twitter, Amway and Kiva show us? They're all examples of what can happen when you build platforms where increasing *observable* consumption creates increasing value for platform users. What happens, though, when something becomes so public it is adopted by everyone at the same time? That's where you start to get the effects of "herd behaviours".

HERD BEHAVIOURS TWIST

During the 1630s, something bizarre happened in Holland: everyone began to believe tulip bulbs – flowers with features quite unremarkable except that they'd become something of a status symbol for the wealthy – were amongst the most valuable commodities in the world.

A tulip bulb takes somewhere between 10 and 12 years to develop from a seed. After that, it produces one flower for one week in every year. It is not, therefore, an especially prolific grower. Because the plant is dormant for so much of the year, individual bulbs can be uprooted and moved around after the flower is produced. This characteristic allowed Dutch traders to write contracts for the future supply of bulbs, in the process inventing the concept of the futures contract.

With increasing demand for the flowers, professional flower growers began to pay higher and higher prices for these contracts, and speculators entered the market. Two years later, the Dutch created a proper futures market for contract trading and prices accelerated.

In 1637, a single tulip bulb sold for more than 10 times the annual income of a skilled craftsman. At one point, in fact, it is said that a whole 12 acres of arable land – a strictly constrained resource in a dyke-surrounded country like Holland – was offered for a single bulb. The rise in prices was driven by a herd behaviour: individuals observed each other paying higher and higher prices for bulb contracts, and recognised that so long as prices continued to rise, there were opportunities to get rich. Since everyone else was making money, they reasoned, they could do so too if they did the same thing.

In February 1637, however, the price stopped going up: the price for futures contracts had gotten so high buyers were spooked. Then, when the traders realised that they had no buyers, the price collapsed, leaving many holding contracts worth a tiny fraction of the price they'd paid.

In retrospect, it is obvious a single tulip cannot be more valuable than the yearly output of 10 craftsmen or worth more than the lifetime production of 12 acres of farmland, so we must ask why a set of otherwise rational business people started to believe it was?

The answer is herd behaviour: the idea that the more a product or service is used, the more likely it is to continue to be acceptable. Where you have a platform where this gets reinforced as consumption increases, a *herd behaviour twist* occurs. In the case of the Dutch, the platform was the invention of futures contracts and the exchanges on which they traded.

Though the Dutch were first to develop herd behaviours on financial platforms, they're quite a regular occurrence. Inevitably, the other examples look as ridiculous in retrospect as the one involving tulip trading.

In 1711 the United Kingdom Government established the South Sea Company, to which it granted a monopoly to trade in Spain's South American colonies. This was part of a treaty agreement, which – amazingly – subsumed the entire national debt of England. The ridiculousness of the South Sea Company was this: the treaty allowed it to send one ship – one ship only – per year to South America. Much was made of the prospects of the company nonetheless, and shares were in feverish demand. In one year, the price went from £100 to £1000, triggering interest from all levels of British society. The collapse, when it came in 1720, bankrupted many.

In the 1840s, herd behaviours caused investors to speculate on the price of railways yet to be built. Over 270 lines were approved by Acts of Parliament, but it soon became apparent that building and operating railways was not as simple or as lucrative as speculators had imagined. Overnight, the price collapsed.

In more recent years, herd behaviours have caused similar

effects. The dot-com bubble of 2000 was the result of fiendish speculation in companies with no inherent value and in 2007, a housing price crash occurred around the world when speculation on the value of mortgages which could not be repaid destroyed the financial system in many countries.

These are stories of ultimately destructive herd behaviours. However, herd behaviour twists can also be advantageous for both customers and vendors. Amazon is a bookstore with a difference: it is a platform that uses the herd behaviours twist to drive purchases of its products. As those who have used the site know, it does this by showing you not only products which you've expressed an interest in, but also those which others like you have expressed an interest as well.

Moreover, Amazon pioneered ratings and reviews as a way to provide consumer insight regarding a prospective purchase. Competing products are categorised by how many stars consumers have given them, and the most purchased products tend to be those with the highest star ratings. Amazon also provides purchasers with the ability to read feedback from other people who have previously bought the product.

Products with many reviews – whether positive or negative – are purchased more frequently than those with few reviews. Why? Because Amazon is a herd behaviours platform – with increasing consumption of a particular product in its store, the platform makes it more likely that others will purchase the product as well.

In 2007, researchers in Taiwan[10] studied this behaviour in an experimental setting by building a bookstore with only two books. In the experiment, participants were asked which of the two books they preferred to purchase, given the star rating other consumers had assigned to each book. Unsurprisingly, books with higher star ratings were purchased more often than those without.

---

10   Chen, Yi-Fi. "Herd Behavior in Purchasing Books Online". Department of International Trade, Chung Yuan Christian University, Taiwan (2007).

But this result masks something more interesting: the number of stars given on average was far less important than the fact that stars existed at all. In other words, books with consumer ratings sold, and those with none, didn't. With this result in hand, researchers dug a little deeper to discover what might be going on. They created a new bookstore, again with only two books in it, but this time providing both expert and ordinary user reviews of each book.

Now, one would intuitively imagine the results would be clear: an expert review of a book would be more likely to influence purchase decisions than the opinions of an uninformed buyer who has written some random review. But in fact, the opposite was true: the experiment demonstrated consumer purchasing preference was hugely influenced by the opinions of other consumers like themselves rather than experts.

If we turn again to the real world of Amazon, we can see the power of the herd behaviour twist in the fortunes of its competitors, the other mail order and retail book operations that existed at the time. Mail order and retail book operations most certainly didn't have any way of exploiting the herd behaviour twist. Their poor substitute was the much less ubiquitous best seller lists, lists which even today account for only a small percentage of the number of books available.

The impact of Amazon on these companies was devastating. Within four years of its founding, Amazon's biggest bricks-and-mortar competitors in the United States, Barnes & Noble and Borders, had started a ruinous price war with the company. Each was discounting up to 50% off the price of new best-selling books to defend their market share. Each has now developed their own online offers to compete with Amazon directly. They both remain in less than rosy financial shape.

Amazon is an example of one of two kinds of herd behaviour twist: one that depends on what academics call an "information cascade". An information cascade occurs whenever many people make the same choice to such an extent it tends to outweigh one's own rational judgement. Customers tend to imagine that "its more likely I'm wrong than all these people, so I will do what they're doing". What arises in these circumstances is convergent behaviour: given individuals face similar decision-making problems, they will likely make very similar decisions.

The other kind of herd behaviour twist is where the platform creates a "path dependency" with increasing use. It is possible to summarise the operation of this twist with two simple words: "history matters". A path dependency happens when the collective choices of a crowd affect the future choices it is possible to make. Essentially, the number of options available in the future is constrained by what's consistent with what's already occured.

Imagine this scenario. As an employer, you decide it is not only sensible, but essential, to force your workers to use a data entry device that's demonstrably the most inefficient possible. It is one that causes repeated strain injuries for a small but significant percentage of the workforce. Moreover, you declare it is the only tool you're willing to have them use, no matter what. This is what's happened with the QWERTY keyboard, used the world over on every kind of computer system.

In 1868, Christopher Sholes (1819–1890) patented the first typewriter, a device with obvious advantages over the handwritten writing it replaced. However, it also had a huge disadvantage: it jammed. Sholes, in attempting to correct this, decided to change the arrangement of the keys on the device's keyboard, ensuring that letters which were most likely to be typed together were put far apart; this was supposed to slow down even the fastest and most able of touch typists, reducing the probability of a jam.

As with all breakthrough inventions, adoption was slow, waiting for the price/performance improvements that would make the device economic for a larger group of users.

Alternative keyboard arrangements were tried as the market grew, though. In 1936 ergonomics professor August Dvorak patented a layout applying everything then known about ergonomic design. The new design was supposedly up to 80 times faster than QWERTY: the US Navy even did a study on the new keyboard to prove its efficiency and found the full cost of retraining a typist on Dvorak's new design was repaid after a mere 10 days. However, this vastly improved performance was not enough to sway typewriter users or manufacturers. Why bother, when everyone had already chosen to use QWERTY? Where was the money going to come from to retrain all those secretaries that were already proficient? Where was the motivation for all those secretaries to change what already worked well for them?

In the end, the choice was already made, and everyone has just stuck with it ever since, perhaps because the bother of changing has been perceived as too great. Once a herd makes a choice to use a particular platform, even the presence of something much better will not sway them, especially when something becomes widely accepted as the normal way of doing things.

This, of course, is the very definition of the consistency with norms innovation attribute Rogers identified in his research. When a twist reinforces this innovation attribute with consumption, each additional user makes it less likely that a competitor will be able to take a position with a simple sidestep. Every time another individual learns QWERTY, the chance it will be replaced with something better is reduced. When was the last time you saw a computer with a different layout?

As an exercise, it is interesting to consider what kinds of innovation would have to arise to actually displace this well-loved keyboard layout, since we've already seen a keyboard arrangement with vastly superior efficiency was insufficient to do so. Clearly, one key attribute would have to be better consistency with norms than QWERTY.

There is probably only one thing that people are more familiar with than typing, and that is speaking. This has not escaped programmers responsible for creating operating systems for computers. All the main ones have rudimentary speech recognition capabilities. At the moment, these are relatively poor substitutes for keyboarding. They're not as accurate as typing, and they often need training before they're much use at all. The present capability is typical for breakthroughs just at the start of the price/performance curve.

One thing is certain though: eventually the price/performance of speech input will improve to the point where it can replace a keyboard. That is a sidestep which will be met with very significant existing demand: there are millions of people trained on keyboards that are potential customers.

Let us turn now to the final kind of single twist, one based on the trialability innovation attribute. When the use of trials expands with consumption, crowds often come up with unexpected results. To start us off, we'll look at one of the most famous crowd examples from the entertainment industry.

EMERGENT WISDOM TWIST

The TV show *Who Wants to be a Millionaire* has been syndicated all over the world. Popular everywhere, the basic premise is this: a guy or girl in the hot seat is asked a series of up to 15 multiple choice questions, each more difficult that the last. Each question is worth progressively more money, and the last is worth one million. Very, very few people have managed to get all the answers correct and win the prize.

The excitement in this game comes when a contestant, with significant sums of money up for grabs, finds they are not sure of the answer. They have the chance to use one of several kinds of lifeline: they can ask that two of the wrong answers be removed.

Or, they can make a phone call to a friend, someone they've pre-nominated as the smartest person they know. Or, most interestingly of all, they can do a spot poll of the audience for the correct answer.

Now, intuitively, you'd expect the friend – the smartest expert the contestants can find – to be right most of the time. Intuition is correct in this case, since analysis shows calling a friend results in a correct answer about 65% of the time. However, calling a friend is much less effective than asking the audience what to do. Contestants who do the latter get the correct answer 91% of the time.

Who Wants to be a Millionaire demonstrates an effect at the heart of the *emergent wisdom single twist*: in creating a platform where consumption increases the value of experimentation and local knowledge, you can create a competitive advantage that's very hard to get around. Sidesteps that use this twist, as we'll see in a moment, are powerful, because each time you trial something, you create local knowledge and experience. When all that adds up across many people, you have a competitive advantage over everyone else, especially when the total sum of all that knowledge is aggregated by a platform.

But aggregating knowledge is only one kind of emergent wisdom twist. The other kind is where all those local trials create coordination and cooperation between individuals who are actually doing something. Have you ever noticed how – in most developed countries – people walk on one side of the pavement or the other? There's very rarely a law in place that causes this kind of thing: people just watch each other and copy the behaviour they see. The result is pedestrian traffic flows more smoothly.

There's an even better example of this to be seen in the UK. For almost all coordinated traffic flows in the country – driving, pedestrian and so forth – everyone coordinates to the left. That's where the slow lane is if you're driving, for example, and you move to the right to overtake.

However, if you want to stand still on an escalator anywhere, you stand on the right, not on the left. There's no rhyme or reason to it: everyone just does it. When you see a tourist arrive from another country, they automatically stand on the left, following the example from every other situation they've experienced. When this happens, all the locals click their tongues and roll their eyes till the "stupid" tourist works out what the crowd wants him or her to do.

I'll give you another example. At my Tube station in London, Goodge Street, there are no escalators, only these big lifts with doors on both sides. Passengers get in one side and exit the other when they get to the surface. Ordinarily, passengers enter and stand facing the way they expect to exit. Everyone does it automatically, and as everyone is packed in like sardines, this seems the best way to respect everyone's personal space. (You'll notice this behaviour in all lifts no matter how many doors there are, actually. Everyone automatically turns to face the exit.)

If, however, the first person to enter the lift turns and faces the other way, quite a few other people do the same thing. They do it instinctively. About every third day, I manage to be the first in the lift and I turn the wrong way, just to prove the emergent wisdom twist works. Next time you're in a lift with two doors, try it yourself.

This sort of behaviour was the subject of a famous experiment in 1960[11]. Researchers set themselves up on a busy street corner in Manhattan. Their first subject was asked to do nothing except stand there and look up into the sky. They then noted how many passers-by looked up as well. The result was interesting. With one person looking up, about 20% of people followed suit. When five people were looking up though, 80% of all other passers-by copied.

---

11   Milgram, S; Bickman, L and Berkowitz, L. Note on the drawing power of crowds of different size. Journal of Personality and Social Psychology 13(2), pp 79–82 (1969).

How does everyone know to stand on the right on the escalator? Why do groups look skywards even when there's nothing to see? The answer is people, when faced with aggregations of information from those around them, will usually arrange themselves to create a coordinated outcome.

Let us look at another example of this in the context of medicine. A clinical trial is the end of a long process of validating a medical treatment option. Basically, a potential medical intervention is tested in a group with a given condition; often, half are given the treatment, and the other half a placebo, in order to see what comparative differences might occur. It is a traditional approach, rooted deeply in formal scientific methodology, and has been the basis of the advancement of medicine for years.

The thing is, clinical trials take a long time. They're horrendously expensive, and they're subject to extraordinary regulatory oversight. All this means it takes years and years for a new treatment option to go from the laboratory to the patient.

But what if there was a better way? What if it were possible for patients to effectively trial treatment options for themselves in such a way that performing more experiments increased the value for everyone else?

It is this basic premise that drove the formation of website CureTogether.com, a place where patients can record the effectiveness of various things they've tried to manage their ailments. When you log in to CureTogether, you're asked to fill in a personal profile in order to baseline some demographic information about yourself. Then, you start telling the site about your medical conditions. For each condition, you can specify a treatment option you've tried, and give a qualitative assessment of its effectiveness. You get to specify the symptoms you're experiencing, and how serious they are. And you get to see what everyone else who has the condition is experiencing and trying as well.

When I first logged into CureTogether, I was personally

interested in treatments for migraine. I don't suffer them very seriously myself – just an annoying headache from time to time, most often triggered by an excess of alcohol and a big night – but my mother finds them debilitating. When she has a migraine, she has to go to bed, block out the light, remove all sound and wait it out. The effects are painful, but more importantly, they affect her work and her quality of life. Doctors who have seen her have tried to prescribe pills, but Mum has always preferred to outlast her migraines.

Over at CureTogether, almost 3,000 people suffer from migraines, many with similar symptoms to those of my mother. Without the cost and delay of a clinical trial, the site found that most people find elimination of red wine, MSG additives from food, extra sleep and being in the dark were by far the most effective treatments; much more effective, in fact, than any of the various recommended medications.

This kind of comparative information would never have been the subject of a clinical trial: someone has to pay, and those who sell treatments are the most likely candidates to do so. "More sleep" is a treatment option that is not likely to have much financial value to a drug company.

CureTogether is an example of a sidestep and twist where the value of the platform increases as the number of experiments increase. It is, actually, one of a whole emerging category of platforms that do this kind of thing, relying on four conditions being present.

The first condition involves individuals having access to private information they can contribute to the crowd. Even if this information is just an eccentric interpretation of facts, it is valuable. That's why increasing trialability in an innovation drives this kind of platform behaviour: trials create local unique knowledge. Your experience with a product or service is likely to be different – in some little way – to the experiences of everyone else who's tried the product.

When all those add up, you get a platform with increasing value. At CureTogether, for example, the sharing of private information is how individual symptoms and treatments have worked. Each person reports their own personal experiences, and it is the sum of these experiences that make the platform valuable.

The second condition required to make an emergent wisdom twist work is the opinions of each individual must be relatively independent. Ideally, you want the local knowledge each trial generates to be unique, because diversity gives the crowd the most information to work with. Alternatively, when you have a crowd that shares a common view, the outcome is largely predetermined by the general consensus.

Obviously, you don't need a crowd to get any insight into the whole if everyone is thinking the same thing: all you have to do ask one person. There would be little point in CureTogether if reactions to disease and response to treatment were identical for everyone. When the outcome is different in some way for each individual, the emergent wisdom twist will create unexpected value, value that's not obvious at the beginning. Who would have thought one of the best preventions for migraine would be getting more sleep?

The third condition enabling an emergent wisdom twist is this: local knowledge must be a practical possibility. People have to be able to specialise, so their experiences are unique. Some products and services don't allow much specialisation; they do one thing, and one thing only. Everyone is guided down the same path, so there isn't much opportunity for individuals to add their unique perspectives and experiences. The product is the product. But when you add hooks that let people contribute unexpected things for themselves, variation begins to develop.

Browsing CureTogether recently, I discovered an unexpected condition: onion intolerance. Apparently, almost 500 people have the condition, and it causes a range of symptoms that range from bloating and flatulence to anaphylaxis. The best treatments for this condition by the way, are: firstly onion avoidance, and secondly reading labels on products to avoid onion additives.

But the real value of the emergent wisdom encapsulated in CureTogether is this: perhaps I don't know I have onion intolerance, but I know something is wrong. So I enter all the symptoms I have, and maybe the site will suggest onion intolerance as the cause. That's certainly emergent wisdom I probably wouldn't have gotten from a drug company or a doctor.

The final condition that needs to be present for an emergent wisdom twist is there has to be some kind of mechanism for turning all this private and localised data into a collective decision, an aggregation mechanism.

Aggregation mechanisms vary widely. For example, the aggregation mechanism for *Who Wants to be a Millionaire* is the automatic voting system that combines the views of everyone in the audience. In CureTogether, the aggregation mechanism is the statistical analysis that summarises treatments, symptoms and illnesses.

What is the common factor for each of these systems though? They each collect individual responses, as soon as the response is available, and represent it in some way that the combined intent of the crowd is made evident.

IN SUMMARY

In this chapter, we've examined how the single twist is able to couple increasing consumption to value. The effects we've been discussing are summarised in Table 4.1 below:

Twist	Behavioural Dynamic	Result
Viral Effects (Observability)	Selfishness	Rewards to individuals improve with consumption
	Altruism	Rewards to groups improve with consumption
Herd Behaviours (Consistency with Norms)	Information cascades	Chance of adoption improves with consumption
	Path dependency	Lock-in of group improves with consumption
Emergent Wisdom (Trialability)	Aggregation	Knowledge of individuals improves with consumption
	Coordination	Behaviour of groups improves with consumption

Table 4.1: Behavioural Dynamics in Single Twists

Now, the value we've examined in this chapter is interesting because it is generated in addition to any that is derived directly from the product itself.

The three innovation attributes considered here – trialability, observability and consistency with norms – are all aspects of product use rather than product *features*. Their effect, when incorporated into a platform, is to bring forward adoption as network effects kick in to help recruitment.

The next question for us to consider is the effect platforms can have on product features, rather than product use. That is the subject of the next chapter, in which we'll examine the double twist in detail.

THE
DOUBLE TWIST

CHAPTER
FIVE

U p to this point, we've concentrated on platforms where the rate of adoption is accelerated with consumption. Increasing observability leads to a viral effects twist, where customers are motivated to recruit other customers. More trials leads to an emergent wisdom twist, where customers discover new knowledge and coordinate new behaviours. And increasing consistency with norms leads to a herd behaviour twist, where customers increase their use of the platform either because they see everyone else doing so, or because their past decisions lead them to do so.

When you build a platform where these attributes get better with consumption, you're able to lock competitors out of your sidestep, no matter how simple the sidestep was to execute. This is because you get the most customers first.

When you have a single twist, the effect is to move the adoption curve to the left as consumption increases. If we refer again to Figure 3.1 (see page 88), we can see this enables a much less developed breakthrough to be successful and/or lets the platform owner charge a price premium.

What a single twist doesn't do, however, is expand the over all market. You may get all the available customers more quickly, but it is the double twist which speeds up adoption and grows the market at the same time.

You'll probably recall from our cursory look at the double twist in Chapter 3 that this happens as either relative advantage is increased or complexity is reduced – or sometimes both. This has the effect of moving the price/performance curve to the left, with the upshot that more potential customers are able to access the innovation economically. As we've seen, this grows the total number of adopters available for a given product. Also, the point of critical mass for the S-curve is much earlier. The result is not only is the market expanded, but growth within the market accelerates at the same time.

How do relative advantage and critical mass vary the price/performance curve? The answer is they change the *intrinsic* features of a product as consumption increases. In other words, as more people adopt, either product capabilities get better, or the price goes down.

This effect is surprisingly common in practice. We come across it, in fact, every time we use any one of the communications technologies we rely on in the modern world: telephone, video conference, email and all the others. These are products whose value improves as their use widens. In this chapter, we'll examine three variations on the double twist. We'll begin with twists where product capability is directly coupled with consumption.

PRODUCTS THAT IMPROVE WITH CONSUMPTION

Let us examine the case of telephony for a moment. Here was a device that took some 50 years to get from the moment of its first practical demonstration to coverage of just under 10% of households in the United States. The reason? At the beginning, the telephone was a practically useless instrument, since so few people used it. The actual device was invented in the 1870s, and was a sidestep from the telegraph.

Telephony seems a natural sidestep – after all, a telegraph is really a way of sending instantaneous written communication, so you'd expect it would be obvious that you'd use the same kind of technology to send spoken words as well. Initially, though, the consuming public was sceptical. Written communication was familiar to everyone, whereas mechanically reproduced sound was something of a novelty.

When Alexander Graham Bell demonstrated a live phone call, it caused awe and wonderment, but most people didn't see much practical advantage in it to start with. After all, you still had to go to the post office or somewhere else where a telephone was installed. That meant making an appointment with whomever you wanted to communicate, since they also had to get to a telephone at the correct time and place. At least telegrams could be delivered by hand, so a new message was of no inconvenience at all to the receiver and didn't require complicated planning in advance.

It took seven years for Bell to create enough interest in his instrument that people were willing to see him lecture on its possibilities. Bell's salespeople were on hand to capture any interest from potential customers, but they faced an uphill battle.

Looking back from the vantage of today, some of the initial objections of customers seem somewhat ludicrous. People wanted to be certain that they couldn't catch any diseases down the electrical wire. Non-English speakers needed to be convinced the telephone could "speak" in their native language. And, people wondered, what would they do with it if they owned one? Initially, telephones were strictly point-to-point, so adoption was limited to those who had regular need to contact specific individuals at a distance. In desperation, Bell's company began to broadcast news, concerts and church services down their wires, just so the telephone could be used for something.

The invention of the telephone exchange greatly increased the value of the telephone, because the instrument was no longer limited by a fixed, point-to-point circuit. Three years later, long-distance services became available: a further enhancement of the price/performance curve. Gradually, the telephone was becoming a useful acquisition for a large number of people.

Adoption of the telephone continued steadily through the innovator and early adopter segments until the early 1940s. At that point, adoption of the telephone took off, reaching critical mass around the same time it was possible to call around the world and manual telephone operators began to disappear. By 2009, 95.6% of United States' households had an active telephone service.

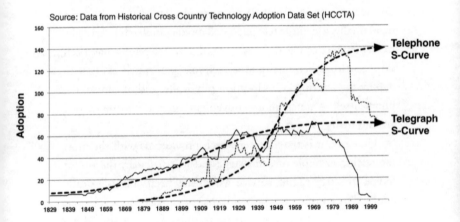

Figure 5.1: Telephone and Telegraph Double Twist

Figure 5.1 shows how the double twist has worked. Telegraphy had a typical adoption S-curve, which took about 140 years to develop from the moment of introduction to the time of peak. Bell introduced his telephone about 50 years later and for the next 50 years or so, the telegraph was still the most important communications technology. Just before World War II, though, telephony took off. You can see how market demand for the telephone accelerated quickly past the penetration of the telegraph. It was a rapid adoption rate which propelled the phone way past the telegraph. The size of the market grew considerably during this process.

The other important point to note in the figure is that instantaneous communication was something most people were familiar with at the time of the telephone's introduction, so it took just 32 years for the phone to reach its peak adoption rate. As expected, the double twist sped up the market and grew it at the same time.

Today, fixed line telephony of the sort invented by Alexander Graham Bell is in decline. The decline is the result of two new technologies: the internet and cell phones. In Figure 5.1, you can see this from about 1986 onwards (at around the time incidentally, use of the telegraph collapsed completely). Actually, in many developing countries, fixed line telephony has been skipped altogether. Cell phone technology is much cheaper to deploy than wiring every location physically, and of course, the phone itself is much more convenient since it can be carried around by its owner.

However, it is the internet which provides us with the most interesting example of a sidestep, and in particular, the rise of Skype, the free calling service which has been enthusiastically adopted by consumers worldwide. Skype is one of those obvious sidesteps that often come up in technology: take something that's working relatively well in the corporate space (the use of digital networks for voice), and shift it to a consumer space with an appropriate modification of the price/performance curve to make it attractive to the home wallet.

In the case of Skype, the price of the service is zero. Consumers can now make long-distance calls for nothing, so long as both parties have the Skype software and an internet connection. Unsurprisingly, moving the price/performance curve to a point where users are able to make calls for free has triggered rapid adoption. Skype is now the largest provider of long distance telephony in the world.

The rise of telephony, and specifically of Skype, demonstrates something that is true for all products that have a double twist: increasing product capability is generated not necessarily because specific features are present, but because those features are used in conjunction with *others*.

What follows from this is simple: double twists where intrinsic product features get better with consumption are inherently social in nature. In almost every case, they depend on some mechanism that enables customers to interact with each other.

ECOSYSTEMS THAT IMPROVE WITH CONSUMPTION

The requirement for direct interactions between customers in order to generate over all capability improvement is generally limited to product categories where communication is at least a subsidiary part of the main value proposition.

There is an alternate way of creating a double twist, though, and that is where the price/performance curve improves as an ecosystem of *complimentary* products develops which are dependent on the main one.

This, of course, is the Microsoft model we examined earlier: by owning more developers than anyone else, and by virtue of the fact that it had more users than anyone else, Microsoft created an effective monopoly in personal computing for the better part of two decades. Microsoft managed to create this situation for itself by ensuring it rushed through critical mass by subsidising Windows (it gave it away to anyone who bought Word or Excel), and then by making sure it had the most developers (Microsoft's developer tools are not only cheap, they are better than anyone else's).

Things, however, have moved on. These days, the new

competitive battleground in personal computing is not the personal computer, but the smart mobile phone, or smartphone. It is a battleground that has recently become very hot indeed. Now, based on its experience, Microsoft could quite easily have expected its tried and tested strategy of sidestepping products with existing demand into this new space would work. This time, it didn't. To understand why, we need to examine the smartphone market and look at the competitive dynamics that have emerged over time.

Presently, in the mobile phone space, there are two kinds of device: feature phones, which consist of any mobile telephone whose primary purpose is making and receiving calls and texts, perhaps with dedicated camera functionality as well. The defining characteristic of feature phones, apart from their low price, is they are generally not platforms that incorporate a double twist. The reason is there are usually few simple ways to upgrade or change their functionality once they have been purchased. In this category, the basis of competition is the number of features that can be shoved into the package at a particular price, rather than any value that's independent of the phone.

The second kind of device has become known as a smartphone. Smartphones are generally much more powerful than feature phones, and importantly, do feature ways to enhance functionality after purchase. Usually, this is through installing applications written by organisations other than the phone's manufacturer. To make this work in a practical way, the phone has to have an operating system program similar to that on personal computers. This, obviously, was fertile territory for Microsoft, given its dominance of other digital platforms.

There had been a few forays into the market of useful smartphones before Microsoft made its first move, however. Palm Computing Corp released the first device, named the Kyocera 6305, a sidestep from the electronic digital assistants the company had pioneered since 1996. It combined diary, contact list and limited web browsing, and was something of a hit, at least in the eyes of journalists on its release in 2001.

In 2002, the then relatively unknown company Research in Motion (RIM) also implemented a sidestep. Initially, RIM were a manufacturer of pager devices they called "Blackberries", a market they did well in, but wasn't growing, since mobile phones now had a ubiquitous replacement: the short message, or SMS service. In an attempt to expand its market, the company decided to try to build something new: a mobile device optimised for email rather than phone calls. This was an obvious move sidestep for a company that had lots of expertise in text-based mobile applications, particularly in applications where security was a significant concern. The new email-optimised Blackberry was a huge commercial success, and racked up tens of millions of subscribers in the first years after its launch.

It was at this point that Microsoft decided to add phone features to its own mobile operating system, Windows CE. Windows CE was a much cut-down version of its standard Windows operating system designed to operate on devices competing in the PDA space. It had a cut-down version of Microsoft Office bundled in and included a set of additional features designed to make switching from a PC running Windows easy.

Microsoft had little experience with phones when it launched its operating system to a largely underwhelmed market, and its first mobile was pretty buggy. It dropped calls randomly. Sometimes it failed to detect that calls were arriving. And users complained that on occasion, the phone just froze, requiring a full reset in order to make it work again.

However, exceptional products have never been the core of Microsoft's strategy. Its success has always been based on exceptional *business* deals. It continued this strategy with Windows for mobile phones. The company licenced its operating system – just as it had done with Windows and MS DOS before – to any manufacturer who wanted to make smartphones. At one stage, reputedly, there were more than 50 handset partners using Microsoft's software, and over 50 million Windows mobile devices were sold in the next few years.

This success was, in part, due to Microsoft's strategy of making things as simple as possible for developers. While consumers had to buy their phone, developers got tools to build software for practically nothing. Microsoft's development tools for phones were, in fact, head-and-shoulders above what anyone else had available at the time, and probably still are. They were cheap, functionally powerful, and most importantly of all, had a long history of development since they'd been used in Windows for over a decade. By contrast, everyone else making smartphones was starting from scratch.

Thus, the scene was set for Microsoft to take control of a new market and in the early days, it looked as if Microsoft was going to repeat its PC-based success. By 2004, Windows Mobile made up 23% of all smartphone sales, and analysts expected that by 2010, it would overtake everyone else and be the undisputed market leader. But just four years later in 2008, its share had declined to only 14%, and by the third quarter of 2009, it held only 7.9% market share.

What went wrong for Microsoft? The short answer is Apple and its iPhone. iPhone was released in 2007 and took the world by storm. Technically, the phone was nothing very special: Apple just sidestepped its decade-old operating system from Macintosh into a new platform with a new interface. But what a sidestep! Apple made *incremental* improvements to the device in almost every way. Firstly, its industrial design was superb. Reviewers, gushing about it, said: "It was the most beautiful industrial design of any phone we've ever seen."[12]

Secondly, Apple attempted to incrementally improve almost every aspect of its first mobile phone. The screen Apple put in the device was better than anything that had come before by quite

---

12   *Engadget*, 3rd July 2007.

a margin. It had a trio of sensors for light, motion and sound, which were all integrated with the functions of the device.

But most importantly, it had a user interface which blended all these features seamlessly. Instead of trying to make Macintosh work on a small screen, Apple built something brand new. Windows for Mobile, on the other hand, attempted to be as familiar to as many people as possible by emulating the PC look and feel as much as possible.

Now, following from our understanding of sidesteps, this should have given Microsoft an advantage, because not only was Microsoft earlier than Apple in the market, it was able to leverage an S-curve from another well-known and very well-adopted product. Microsoft were very confident their position in the market was safe, and, in any case, they'd defeated Apple before using a strategy fundamentally the same as the one they were employing now. They were so confident that Steve Ballmer, Microsoft's CEO, actually came out and said how unlikely Apple was to succeed.

Speaking in a live video interview shortly after the launch of the iPhone, Ballmer made the point that Microsoft were selling millions of smartphones a year, whilst Apple were selling none. Furthermore, he went on, at the price Apple wanted to charge for their new device, they'd have the most expensive phone in the market for a long time to come.

Ballmer knew what he was talking about, since Apple *did*, in fact, have one of the most expensive phones in the marketplace. And he knew a thing or two about getting new things adopted, since he'd personally been involved in getting both MS-DOS and Windows to critical mass. In Ballmer's experience, subsidies and bundles to build market share had always been a successful strategy.

But in the first year of sales, Apple managed to secure 6.5% of the total smartphone market worldwide, despite its price, and despite the fact there was no ecosystem of complimentary products available. Somehow, Microsoft's well-tested sidestep and twist-based competitive barriers weren't working. Microsoft may have had more users and more developers, but was losing share regardless. Actually, Apple didn't even let developers write software for iPhone at the start. If the definition of a smartphone is that you can add features after you've bought it, the initial iPhone was only marginally in the same league as Windows Mobile.

What on earth could possible be going wrong for Microsoft? The answer was although people had the *capability* to install new features on their Windows Mobiles, few were actually doing so. Frankly, the processes involved put most people off. You had to plug your phone into a computer, hunt around the internet for software you wanted to use, mutter a few magic incantations, and then hope the installer process would work. It often didn't, and over-the-air installation of software was something most handset manufacturers couldn't achieve successfully. Because few people were actually using custom software on their Windows Mobile devices, Microsoft's investments in getting to a critical mass of users and developers were largely irrelevant.

It was then Apple launched its killing blow, the App Store. Here was a sidestep and double twist that permanently upset the mobile phone applecart. Apple sidestepped its model for selling music on iPod into the phone market by creating a retail environment in which application developers could sell and distribute their wares to phones with itself as the only platform provider. App Store is, essentially, a mechanism that enables Apple to move the price/performance curve for iPhone to the specific point that optimises the chances of adoption.

Because the universe of possible applications you can access is so large, there is always something there for every user, which makes the phone more useful. Apple even played on this factor when it launched a major advertising campaign focussing on the App Store, running the tag line: "There's an App for that!".

Figure 5.2 shows how the introduction of the App Store boosted the iPhone to a new level of sales that it would have been unlikely to achieve so early without. App Store came out in the third quarter of 2008, and by the end of the year, had added almost 4 million devices to the shipment volume of iPhone.

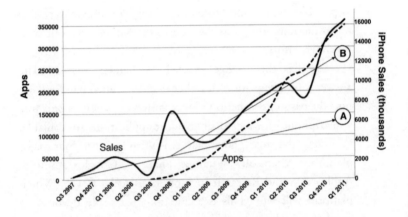

Figure 5.2: iPhone Apps available versus iPhone Sales

In the figure, the projected sales *prior* to App Store is shown as the line marked A. From the third quarter of 2008 onward, the twist effect from the App Store changes the sales trajectory (line B) by expanding the available market and accelerating demand. Also note the widening gap in the "jaws" between these two lines: in other words, as the number of applications for iPhone expands, so too does demand.

The introduction of App Store on iPhone has had an incredible effect on the way the smartphone market is structured. In the past, smartphone features were predominantly aimed at business users. Since App Store, the marketplace has been ruled by consumer consumption. Business users have the kinds of resources at their disposal to work their way through complicated and difficult installs of additional software on phones. Either they have a technology organisation that does it for them, or the relative advantage of using applications on a smartphone is so compelling they will put up with the challenges of getting things to work.

The consumer market, on the other hand, has little access to help. They rely on making things work with as little bother as possible. When App Store came along, consumers were able to do the same things as their business counterparts, but with much less effort.

How has this change affected the handset market? The answer is mobile platforms, rather than individual handsets, are now the basis of competition, since customers will now only buy a smartphone on which their favourite applications are available.

Today, the smartphone market is separated into four major platforms: Microsoft's Windows Phone 7, Google's Android, Apple's iOS and Research In Motion's Blackberry OS. Which platform will win? This is a question that really devolves to another: which company has the best strategy for gaining the most users, and therefore, which will have the most developers to write applications?

We will return to this question in the next chapter, where we discuss strategic applications of the sidestep and twist.

LOCALITIES THAT IMPROVE WITH CONSUMPTION

There is one further variation of the double twist. In both cases we've looked at so far, the over all value of the proposition improves as consumption increases, either because the product itself got better, or because some ecosystem around the product got better.

The remaining case for us to examine is where consumption improves the over all value of the platform, but for each customer, the amount of value generated is localised by a much smaller subset of people than that associated with the whole platform.

Often, these kinds of double twists are associated either with social or geographical locality. In the former case, value is generated by how many of the people you know are using the platform, and increases with social proximity. In the latter, value comes from features of the platform that relate to the physical location of the customer.

Probably the best example of a locality double twist is the success of Facebook, where value is generated because the platform enables social interaction between people who are socially close to each other, especially family and friends.

The story of the rise of Facebook is an interesting one to us in another way as well, because it illustrates the power of the double twist to bestow competitive advantage. That's because the story of the rise of Facebook is *also* the story of the fall of MySpace, which immediately preceded it as the king of social networks.

Both FaceBook and MySpace are online social networks. They were not, however, the first online sites to explore the potential of locality based double-twists. That honour goes to another site which pioneered connection-making between real-world friends. The site, Friendster, launched in 2002, and was immediately very popular: by the end of the first three months of operation, it had 3 million users, which was about one in every 126 users of the internet at the time.

But Friendster's reign as the darling of the internet was not to last long: the following year, 2003, a group of employees at Los Angeles-based online media company, eUniverse, decided to "clone" its features and launch a site of their own. The new site, MySpace, took less than 10 days to build, and its first customers were all employees of eUniverse.

Knowing that acquisition of a decent user base was the only way it was going to succeed – especially considering Friendster had already achieved a critical mass of users – the company began to hold contests to see which of its employees could sign up the most new members. The contest strategy was successful, but the company was still trailing behind Friendster.

Throwing all caution to the wind, eUniverse used a list of 20 million email addresses to spam-mail every account it could get its hands on. Only 5% of the emails resulted in a member for MySpace, but those one million users were enough to achieve critical mass. The double twist kicked into action. Nine months later, MySpace had five million users and surpassed Friendster as the leading social network online.

What was it about MySpace that made it so popular? Unlike rival sites, such as Friendster, MySpace quickly recognised that in addition to functionality that allowed people to connect with each other, there had to be something to do once people were connected. So eUniverse made each MySpace profile a blank canvas, and every member could use their creative energy in any way they liked to reflect their interests and personalities.

All this freedom made MySpace an attractive place for indie bands and film producers to hang out. It was also popular with teenagers who, having grown up with internet tools and SMS texting on their phones, were looking for an online space they could claim for their own. These groups synergised, each driving and expanding adoption in the way that twists almost always do.

Meanwhile, Friendster made significant mistakes. It failed to recognise the lack of control at MySpace was a significant attraction for users, and tightly restricted what users could do on their profile pages. In some cases, it even went so far as to *expel* bands and users for not complying with its profile page standards. If that weren't bad enough, rumours sufaced that Friendster was considering charging for use. Migration to MySpace accelerated. MySpace continued to grow as its double twist kicked in and the product got better with consumption. By the end of 2006, it had more than 80 million users. Two years later, it had grown to 115 million, but adoption was slowing quickly. Something had gone wrong, something unexpected.

The something unexpected was Facebook, a site that significantly changed the price/performance curve for social networks *and* simultaneously attacked MySpace's core user demographic in an extremely interesting and innovative way. How did Facebook, a website that started out as a dorm room prank, manage to achieve this? As anyone who has watched the film *The Social Network* will know, it managed it by starting out in an ultra-niche, and expanded from there.

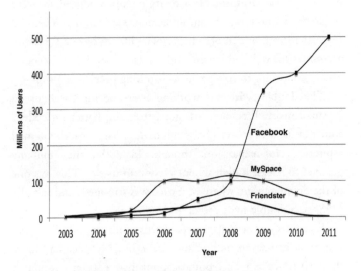

Figure 5.3: Adoption of Internet Social Networking

Facebook initially targeted college students at Harvard. Launched in February 2004, it came along a year after MySpace, which by then already had millions of users. Because of the double twist incorporated in MySpace, it had no practical chance of unseating it in any head-to-head competition. But what it could do was be the number one social network in its niche, something Facebook achieved in less than a month, by which time more than half the undergraduate population of Harvard were using the site. The next month, Facebook opened its doors to students at Stanford, Columbia and Yale, where it experienced similar rapid uptake. The remaining Ivy League schools in the United States followed, with other higher institutions across the country on-boarding as well.

By 2005, almost 85% of undergraduate students on campuses supported by Facebook were using the site. It was still closed: you had to have a student account with an .edu address to get access. But almost *everyone* with an address at a supported institution was using it; 60% of its members logged in every single day without fail. Soon, it became essential, if you wanted to participate in much of college social life, to have a Facebook account. One well-publicised study, in fact, found that Facebook was as important to college life as drinking beer[13].

The double twist was working overtime for Facebook in its small niche. Facebook just got better and better for college students as greater numbers came on board. Facebook had aspirations for expansion, though. In 2005, the company decided to release a high school version of its site. This was one of the demographics where MySpace was strongest, and initially MySpace's double twist protected it.

Facebook's growth appeared, at this point, to stall. By 2006, Facebook had seven million members, but MySpace had more than 10 times as many. But Facebook had a secret weapon: it was based on a "locality" double twist. MySpace, on the other hand, wasn't.

With Facebook, you only get updates from those people in your personal social network. You have to actually *know* the people well enough to link up with them by email before you can add them. This was in contrast to the other social networks of the time, which allowed you to link with anyone you liked. MySpace had 100 million users, but the value of the

---

13   Student Monitor's Lifestyle and Media Study, 2006.

connections between each of these users was low. By contrast, each connection on Facebook was incredibly valuable: they were real social connections that got used for real social activity.

In September 2006, Facebook decided to make active use of these valuable connections by launching a feature called News Feed. With News Feed, every time a user gave a status update, uploaded a photo, or did anything else on the site, a broadcast update was posted to everyone else in their social network. MySpace had nothing similar available and was unable to respond.

At the end of 2006, Facebook decided to open its doors to anyone with a valid email address, after a successful closed trial in several companies proved there was demand outside college campuses. Unlike its previous foray into high schools, this caused adoption to sky-rocket. By January 2007, Facebook had doubled its user base.

Now Facebook faced a new problem. It was growing, though still trailed MySpace by a huge margin. MySpace still had the member advantage, so much more content was being created there than anywhere else, including Facebook. Though Facebook was bringing new customers to social networks, adults who'd never been signed up to a social network before, the problem was they didn't have much to do once they'd arrived except share photos and give status updates. On MySpace, at least, you could blog, and create other sorts of content.

Facebook then launched what would turn out to be the killer blow. It decided it would launch an *ecosystem double twist* by allowing people to build new applications that would use its valuable network connections between its users. The Facebook Platform, when it launched on 24 May 2007, used News Feed and all the other mechanisms of the locality double twist to devastating effect. Every time you used a new application, all the people in your social network were notified. Every single app that launched on Facebook initially exploded in usage. Their owners were forced to start frantic searches for new server capacity as loads spiked. News Feed coupled with all those valuable social connections made everyone use *everything*.

From 2006 to 2008 Facebook and MySpace engaged in a war of attrition, where each fought to have the most members. Facebook dramatically expanded the number of things that its users could do with their social network via applications, with viral distribution guaranteed by newsfeeds. And MySpace responded by adding new content. It wrote the biggest number of licence deals with music labels and added portal features around jobs, lifestyle and news. It even launched in-web TV channels and radio stations.

The MySpace strategy was a very traditional one: namely, stitch up the rights to all things members might want to do or see in order to ensure they'd have little motivation to go elsewhere. Facebook, on the other hand, made it possible for *its* members to enhance the Facebook product for themselves, and made sure that everyone could see what everyone else was doing. By mid-2007, reports indicated that MySpace users were migrating to Facebook.

Unsurprisingly, it was the kids leaving high school for college that were moving over. This was worrying for MySpace, but the site was still in a dominant position. After all, Facebook had only 30 million members compared to the 100 million MySpace could claim. But a problem for MySpace was looming. Its growth, despite its incredibly strong assets, was flat. Content, it seemed, wasn't the draw card the site had expected. Facebook, on the other hand, was still growing rapidly as users found more things they could do with their localised social networks.

By April 2008, Facebook surpassed MySpace altogether. Most of this growth came from international markets, rather than the United States. MySpace began to haemorrhage. Members were leaving because by now Facebook had a wide variety of intelligent and useful applications, whilst MySpace had begun to stagnate around two categories: music and messaging. MySpace's initial freedom and lack of format control features – features which had initially helped it defeat Friendster – were now a source of irritation to members, who found the site difficult and confusing to navigate.

By the start of 2011, MySpace was losing nearly 10 million users a month. Then, in March that year, its chief executive, Mike Jones, had to concede defeat saying: "MySpace is no longer a social network" and that "it is now a social entertainment destination".

There is a key lesson to be learnt from this story, of course, and it is this: not all double twists are created equal. Facebook was based on a locality double twist – the product improved as the *personal* social network of its users increased. Each time Facebook adds a new member, the social life of someone, somewhere, gets a bit better. MySpace, on the other hand, got better as more people in general joined. However, the incremental value for each individual member wasn't as great, because, often, the links between members had little value themselves.

AND IN CLOSING

We've explored how the double twist operates to expand the market whilst simultaneously speeding up adoption. We've also seen how such twists operate either at a product, ecosystem or local level to enhance the price/performance of a product as consumption improves. It should be obvious a double twist has more potential upside for organisations than a single twist as a result of its twin action on both the S-curve and price/performance curve.

Less obviously, however, one ought to consider double twists pitted against each other. A product that improves with consumption is one thing. More powerful, however, is the idea of an ecosystem that improves with consumption. With this type of twist, there is more rapid improvement in the price/performance curve, because the opportunity for interesting applications based on the core platform expand each time a new complimentary product is added. Ecosystem twists allow customers to personalise their usage to the specific price/performance point that works for them, and the size of the ecosystem is the key determinant of their ability to do so.

However, the most powerful kind of double twist is based on localities. Localities are so powerful because they are specific and personal to a customer from the moment they're established. Customers find them so compelling because they offer a price/performance curve which is the most efficient possible at an individual level. All the other twists, in contrast, tend to aggregate their value at a much larger group level.

With the discussion of twists complete, it is time to turn our attention to questions of practicalities: namely, the set of considerations needed when building a product based on the sidestep and twist. These considerations are the subject of the next chapter.

BUILDING A SIDESTEP AND TWIST

CHAPTER SIX

The kinds of business we've been examining in the latter pages of this book are quite a far cry from those of yesteryear. In those days, breakthroughs had every chance of creating very great wealth. Why were breakthroughs so profitable then, and not now?

The simple answer is that two centuries ago efficient resource utilisation was the only competitive advantage that mattered. It was breakthroughs such as the steam engine that created massive efficiencies in a very short time. With a steam engine, you might work a shallow mine, previously abandoned because of flooding. You could mass-produce textiles where only cottage industries had existed previously. Or, you could move people and goods in a fraction of the time over great distances, removing the limitation of the distance a horse could travel in a day.

Efficient resource allocation created a boon for those smart enough to take advantage of it. If you had more factories, more people, and more money than your competitors, you were likely to get richer, no matter how poorly conceived the product or service. More recently, the attention of corporate strategists has switched from *resource* control to *information* control. In almost every respect, economies based on information control are little different to those they supersede.

Companies are still engaged in competitive battles, but they're based on the notion of winning by denying access to key *knowledge* needed to produce things rather than control of the raw materials themselves. We have labelled this new system of doing business the "knowledge economy", but it has more similarities with the industrial age than it might first appear.

The number one similarity in both economic systems is based on the premise that only when things are scarce are they worth any money. As I argued in Chapter 3, the mechanisms the knowledge economy uses to support a price for information are failing in our modern, ultra-connected times. Crowds of people, coordinated by the internet, are able to get around such restrictions without much difficulty.

If the fundamentals of the knowledge economy are beginning to unwind, what is emerging to replace it? If you examine the most successful companies today, their advantages derive neither from control of resources nor from control of knowledge. Instead, they are good at something new: building and running processes to deliver product after product, based on their particular core competencies. Apple has done it repeatedly by focussing on design. Amway managed its distribution network of re-sellers, rather than concentrating on making new products. Google does it by concentrating on search facilities and making information accessible. The niche rock band Dispatch filled Madison Square Garden by concentrating on live performances, rather than recording contracts.

This is a list which extends to every case we've looked at in these pages. Companies take what's already well known and sidestep. Then they either single or double twist to make sure no one else can compete.

Of course, the sidestep and twist is different for every company and every product, which brings us to the point of this chapter: what are the key things to consider if you want to build a sidestep and twist for your product?

WHEN TO SIDESTEP?

To start, it is useful to revisit the sidestep. Sidesteps are about making choices that offer a variation of an existing price/performance curve so the product can attract new customers in an existing market, or moving the entire price/performance curve to an aligned market.

To decide on the best strategy, one examines the future prospects of a product in terms of its price/performance curve over time. Now, the normal trajectory is for price/performance of a breakthrough to improve as a result of multiple sidesteps.

At the beginning, this tends to be dramatic because incremental improvements arrive in quick succession. In Figure 6.1 (opposite), you'll see this at point A, which is the point where a breakthrough is introduced to a market. The price/performance at this point is relatively poor. It is very expensive to adopt the breakthrough for the amount of functionality it provides. Economically speaking, this limits the target market to those customers with a particularly specialised need.

Historically, for genuine technological breakthroughs, such markets have traditionally been the military-industrial complex and large corporations, who have deep, deep pockets. Radar, computers, aircraft, microwaves and all the more recent technological achievements of the current century weren't consumer products initially: when they were invented, they were genuinely new. They were consequently expensive, didn't work that well, and were certainly not well tuned enough that an untrained consumer might use them effectively. This is why, around point A in Figure 6.1, there are very few options for sidesteps.

There is little point in increasing functionality and price, since such specialised customers who may be targeted at this price/performance level are so few that further specialisation makes little sense. On the other hand, it is likely the function set of a breakthrough – since it is so new – is not amenable to removal of functionality to *reduce* the price/performance either.

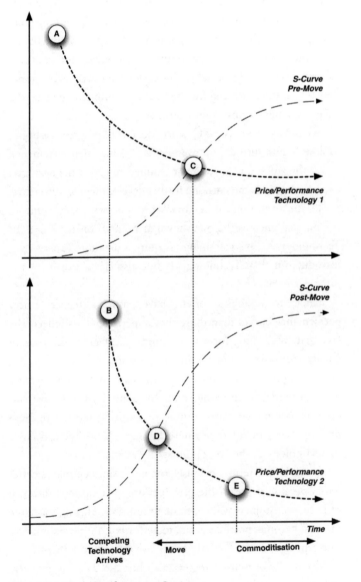

Figure 6.1: Price/Performance Options

However, the pace of improvement is fast. As improvements come along, it becomes much simpler to vary the price/performance curve by adding or removing features to maximise the total market. This is the optimum strategy for product managers at all times between point A and point C on the figure. Such an impressive rate of improvement does not continue forever, however. Eventually, the easiest improvements, those that return the best bang for the buck, get implemented, so the pace of change begins to slow down.

We can see this at point C, where the rate of progress has begun to slow. Whilst further improvement is possible, their incremental cost – the amount of investment required to get to the next level of performance – starts making further development less attractive.

In the meantime, other breakthroughs will have come to the market, such as the one shown at point B on the curve for Technology 2. This technology is quite a bit more expensive at introduction than Technology 1, but also has a much steeper price/performance curve.

Later technologies often have much steeper price/performance curves than those they supersede. This reflects the fact that, over time, for a given product category, the pace of change tends to speed up. Technology 2 is still well before its peak rate of improvement. Since that's the case, it has significantly more potential in the long term. By point C, firms have two options: companies can continue maximising returns through dis/improvement sidesteps on Technology 1; or they can move to Technology 2, shown at point D.

In the longer term, obviously, the move sidestep makes better sense, because it means the price/performance options they can offer their customers will continue to improve. Having made the move, it becomes possible, again, to perform multiple dis/improve sidesteps to optimise S-curves to achieve maximum returns.

Eventually, of course, progress in Technology 2 begins to slow as well, something that occurs at point E. What should firms do then?

Once again, there are two options. Firstly, there may be another technology that can be sidestepped into the market to continue the rapid improvement in price/performance. If so, it makes sense to make another move sidestep to continue the downward trend.

What happens, though, if there is no available technology for a move? In this case, the firm should consider planning to deal with a market in which the basis of competition will shift from delivering new value to customers through improvements in performance to one where value is delivered through improvements in *price*. In other words, at point E, unless a further sidestep is available or there is some kind of competitive barrier, the product is going to become commoditised.

In a moment, we'll examine twists in the light of their value by the time a technology reaches point E. First, let us see how all this has worked in the real world example of computer hardware, where successive introductions of technology have created astounding increases in price/performance. Table 6.1 illustrates how this happened over the last 50 years.

Paradigm	Approximate Peak Price/ Performance Year*	Start Price/ Performance*	Best Price/ Performance *
Electro-mechanical	1930	0.000001	0.0001
Relay	1940	0.01	0.01
Valve	1955	0.01	50
Transistor	1968	1	1000
Integrated circuits	Not at peak	1,000	> 100,000,000

* Number of calculations per second for each US$1,000 investment
Adapted from data by Ray Kurzweil

Table 6.1: Computing Technology Sidesteps

Computers, in their first incarnations, were nothing at all like those we use today. The earliest examples were largely electro-mechanical and included devices such as weaving looms that used punched cards to control the patterns. These mechanisms used electricity and moving parts to perform rudimentary calculations, and at the peak of their development, their price/performance was about one calculation per second for every million dollars invested. In other words, very expensive. Of course, with such poor price/performance characteristics, the promise of computing was hardly going to be realised in any substantial way so inventors quickly moved onto a new technology: the electro-magnetic relay. The relay was a device that had been used successfully for telegrams and telephones, so it was well understood, and more importantly, readily available to early computer scientists. The sidestep was obvious.

Essentially, a relay is a switch controlled by an electro-magnet. When you apply a current, the switch closes. Since computers are built using various combinations of switches tied together, the first real computing machines used them to automatically perform calculations and store results. One of the first machines that did this was built by German student Konrad Zuse (1910–95), as a doctoral project in his parent's lounge. The computer weighed over a thousand kilograms, used hundreds of relays, and was able to perform only a single addition operation every five seconds. If you wanted multiplication, it took twice as long as that.

As you can see in Table 6.1, computers based on relays didn't undergo much improvement in their price/performance characteristics. The reason is simple: mechanical switches still have to move to operate, so to speed up computation the only strategy available is to reduce the size of the switch. Early computer scientists approached physical limitations very quickly, because the high voltages they employed jumped easily between contacts as they made their switches smaller.

Inventors were forced to find something else if they wanted to continue to advance their designs. It wasn't long before they began to try experiments with electronic valves. Valves – an enhanced version of the technology that John Ambrose Fleming invented – don't use mechanical movement. Instead, they're based on the idea that electrical currents can control currents – an effect Fleming used to create the first wireless telegraph. In computers, this is used to make a switch, a switch that can operate much more quickly than a relay since there are no moving parts.

The first valve computers appeared in 1942. These new machines were something of a state secret (which is often the case for breakthroughs, particularly when they are at the start of their price/performance continuum), and most of the interesting early applications were military. At Bletchley Park just north of London, for example, the UK government created a super-secret computer system called Colossus, which it used to break German codes.

The first version of Colossus, which became operational in 1944, used 1500 valves, and two years later, was rebuilt with more capability using 2400. The Colossus computers were all destroyed in 1945 by order of Winston Churchill, who demanded they be broken into "pieces no bigger than a man's hand". Consequently their extraordinary role in the war – some have suggested the machines shortened it by at least two years – didn't really become known until the 1970s. Colossus, and all other computers based on valves, were significantly superior to those that went before, as you can see in Table 6.1.

By the time valves reached the end of their price/performance curve in 1955, US$1000 could buy you nearly 50 calculations a second, and computers had begun to be used commercially, in addition to their important ongoing roles in scientific and military applications.

But some fundamental limitations of valves never went away, and they were these: in order to work, they needed lots of power, and much of that power was converted into heat. As the density of the components increased (a necessary thing in order to make faster and more powerful computers), the valves got harder to keep cool, and their power demands got more excessive. With that, came problems with reliability. As with the relay-based computers that preceded them, it wasn't long before designers began to run into physical limitations.

Luckily, a new technology was developing rapidly: the transistor. A transistor does everything a valve can do, but is made from a tiny piece of silicon. Transistors didn't heat up, can work with low voltages, and, most importantly, were *small*. Small enough you could put 10 or more into the same space occupied by a single valve.

Transistorised computers rapidly emerged. The first, which became operational at the University of Manchester in 1953, used (eventually) 200 transistors and 1300 diodes, and consumed about 150 watts of power. That's just a bit more than a domestic light bulb. By contrast, the Manchester University valve-based machine it replaced used 25 kilowatts, the same amount of power consumed by present-day experimental military lasers that can knock missiles out of the sky. Transistorised improvements brought a dramatic improvement in price/performance: at their peak, a computer could be had which could perform a calculation a second for each dollar invested.

But the pace of advancement continued to increase, and by 1968, computer scientists were again approaching physical limits. This time, they discovered their computers started going wrong as they added more transistors, because the machines were becoming so fast that signals couldn't move quickly enough between individual transistors. Even though electrical signals travel at the speed of light, problems arise when you have thousands that must be coordinated to arrive at precisely the same moment. The difficulty arose because the time electricity was taking to travel on the wires *between* each transistor began to be a factor that needed to be designed around.

There was only one answer, and that was to dramatically shrink the distances between each component. To answer this new challenge, Nobel Prize winner Jack Kilby of Texas Instruments dreamed up the integrated circuit, now known colloquially as a "chip". Instead of manufacturing separate transistors and connecting them with wires, Kilby put multiple transistors on each piece of silicon, embedding the wires directly. It resulted in a massive reduction in the distance between components, and led directly to the computers we use today.

Computers based on chips have driven an explosion in performance. By 2000, the price/performance of computers had grown by several orders of magnitude over transistors: a dollar could buy 100,000 calculations per second. And the rate of improvement has continued: every year, the price/performance ratio of computers has more than doubled.

Now, whilst the price/performance of computer chips has presently not peaked, it is already possible to see how even this technology will need to be replaced by something in due course. Scientists now build components so small on chips that specific molecular level interactions have to be taken into account in their designs. Components that small have random characteristics that are very hard to deal with, and the smaller you go, the more you have to design around the molecular chaos that underlies all matter.

If current trends continue, analysts have estimated that present-day methods of manufacturing chips will reach hard physical limits around 2019. Already, though, there are new computing paradigms on the horizon to replace silicon. Quantum, optical, multicore and other techniques are all potential replacements. Is there anything to suggest the cycle of sidesteps will somehow stop for computing technology? Not at all, at least in the medium term.

BUILDING A TWIST

In Figure 6.1 (see page 161), at point E, we have a situation where the natural market tendency is to switch from competition based on price/performance to competition based *entirely* on price alone. By this time, there are few alternatives available to firms *except* to compete on a price basis, unless they have found some way to constrain supply and/or lock out entrants. One way to do this, as I've argued earlier, is to ensure you control critical inputs: i.e., either the resources needed for production, or the knowledge needed to utilise those resources.

However, this book has been about a third option: building platforms where increasing consumption creates competitive barriers that make it difficult for anyone else to sidestep. In Figure 3.1 (page 88) and Figure 3.2 (page 92) again, the twists all have one thing in common: they rely on getting to a critical mass point before they're effective. Critical mass, in this case, means the intersection of the price/performance curve on the supply side, and the adoption S-curve on the demand side.

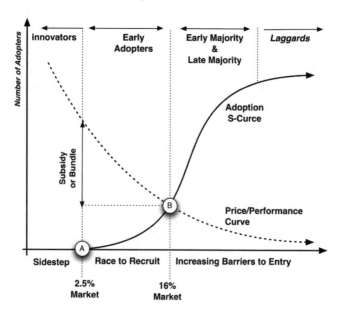

Figure 6.2: Phases for Building a Twist

However, it is by no means a simple task to build a twist, and Figure 6.2 illustrates the reason why. As we know already, twists work by expanding value as consumption increases. Logically then, when the product first appears, there is no consumption, and therefore the amount of value on offer is much less significant than it will eventually become. We see this at point A on the figure.

However, the situation is actually much more difficult than it first appears. That's because at the start of any S-curve, the only people who are interested in a brand new product are those in the *innovator* category: individuals with such tolerance for risk they'll try any new thing once, even if no one around them can give them any evidence that its worthwhile doing so.

Here is the conundrum: most of the value for a product with a twist will arise only when lots of people have started using it. But the innovator segment has to be convinced to try the product *on its own merits,* without the benefit of any of the features that will later arise due to network effects. This is a chicken-and-egg problem of the first order, one made more difficult because this is also the point where the price/performance curve of the new product is at its most unattractive.

It is not, however, one that is insoluble. Both Apple with iPhone and Alexander Bell with the telephone successfully solved the problem, and both did it by deliberately sidestepping an innovator segment into the product from elsewhere. Apple, if you'll recall, was the subject of ridicule by Steve Ballmer of Microsoft, who made the point that the company would have the most expensive phone in the market, and was therefore unlikely to sell many units. But what Ballmer failed to take into account was Apple was able to sidestep demand from the loyal base of its customers who already had iPods and Macs.

These were people who already had Apple products, some of which already did quite a bit of what an iPhone could do. For example, if you had an iPod, you were already familiar with how the music ecosystem that Apple had built was going to work on the iPhone. The risk involved in trying the new device was, therefore, much reduced. (Queues formed outside Apple Stores to buy the iPhone when it finally became available some six months after the launch date was announced.)

Bell solved his chicken-and-egg problem in the same way. By playing live music and events down the phone wires, he was able to sidestep demand from an audience already very familiar with the gramophone and recorded reproduction of sound. In both cases, the sidestep worked to bring demand from some other product category in the critical innovator segment. Doing this forms the establishment phase for the twist.

From our understanding of S-curves, we know the innovator segment of any particular market is about 2.5% of the total. Can a mere 2.5% of a market drive twist-based effects to start the value process off? It depends on the product, as you'd expect. However, an innovator segment does enable the recruitment of the early adopter segment of the market in order obtain a foothold that can drive mass adoption.

How did Facebook unseat its much more powerful rival MySpace? It actively recruited college students from across the United States in order to build a critical mass. In fact, it raced to recruit them, knowing that each campus was a separate battle it needed to win if it was to succeed.

This is the next phase involved in building a twist. It is a race to get as many users as possible, a race to reach critical mass in the shortest time frame. For Facebook, the race was complicated because there were other powerful competitors with established network effects in play. MySpace, in particular, had a much greater number of users; but though the social network was broad in scope, its real hard core was comprised of bands, their music and the people who were interested in them. Facebook would likely have had little chance to compete against this behemoth if it had decided to battle head-to-head for the same audience, but as we know, it chose its own niche and expanded from there.

Once a significant body of the innovator segment has tried (and stayed) with a product based on a twist, the strategic challenge becomes using this beach-head to recruit early adopters. Early adopters aren't *quite* so tolerant of risk as their innovator predecessors, but they'll be willing to try new things *if* the benefits of the product are right and they can a see a few usage examples on which they can base their own decision-making process.

Once again, this is something of a chicken-and egg-problem. Because most of the product's benefits will arrive only *after* the critical mass point, since that's the time network effects really start to kick in, the price/performance of the product will not likely have changed much from that offered to the innovator segment. Yet, this category of users is somewhat more risk averse than the innovators, so are unlikely to adopt unless something is done to improve the value proposition to balance this out.

There are only a few options available. You can reduce the price or you can improve the functionality. Or, in some cases you can do both. The point of doing this is to artificially advance the price/performance curve to the point where critical mass can occur (see point B in Figure 6.2). Artificial advancement is necessary because only at point B are there sufficient numbers of people willing to sign up to the product that critical mass becomes possible.

Reducing the price – essentially subsidising the product – is a strategy we've already discussed in some detail. Ideally, one subsidises the demand-generation side of the market, those that have the most influence on the money side, in order to drive adoption. But the other strategy available is to improve *performance*.

Now, the ordinary course of introducing sidesteps all have the effect of addressing this, but as we can see in Figure 6.2, this takes time. Since building a twist is actually a race to recruit, it is often a good idea to artificially improve the performance of a product.

The easiest strategy for doing so is to bundle one product with another – a strategy we've seen played out in many of the case studies in this book. Microsoft, for example, artificially improved the price/performance of Windows by handing it out for free with copies of Word and Excel when they needed to drive demand to their platform. They went on to artificially enhance the price/performance of Internet Explorer by bundling in the operating system. And subsequently, they've adopted the same strategy for any number of other products as well. In almost every case they've done so, the result has been that Microsoft has been able to get to the critical mass point quickly. The rest, as they say, has been history.

In Figure 5.3 (see page 149), this is exactly the strategy Facebook adopted, too. Prior to 2007, the company was experiencing a fairly standard growth rate: it was essentially doing lots of hard work to win users away from MySpace. Afterwards, though, adoption skyrocketed.

With its release of the Facebook platform (its ecosystem double twist), the company created a massive opportunity for organisations to bundle their unique intellectual property with the functionality already on Facebook. Each time some organisation did so, it made the value proposition of Facebook better; or, in other words, improved the price/performance ratio.

Bundling and subsidises are, actually, two sides of the same coin. Both have the effect of making a product more attractive to the group of people who are unable to adopt economically *until* the critical mass point is reached. The critical mass point happens when a product has gained somewhere around 16% of the total market available. Once critical mass has been achieved, network effects kick in, and active recruitment by the platform operator can reduce or cease.

It is usually safe to conclude, at this point, that competitors' sidesteps will have negligible effects on returns for the remainder of the product's life. In order to compete, in fact, the competitors' sidestep would need to be backed with a twist of its own. This is not impossible, as we've seen in the competition between MySpace and Facebook, but it is difficult. After all, Facebook had to create two double twists in order to win, in the end. Most companies are lucky to have one!

SINGLE TWIST DESIGN

Single twists are based on the idea that network effects can do much more than traditional thinking about them normally suggests. That's because most people imagine network effects in terms of specific product functionality, which get better as consumption increases.

Earlier, we saw how three attributes of innovations – trialability, observability and consistency with norms – can also lead to network effects when integrated into a platform.

What remains, then, is gaining an understanding of the specific features of platforms that need to be present in order to ensure these kinds of network effects kick in. It is the purpose of Table 6.3 to provide a summary of these product features. As you can see, the thing that's common to all single twists is there is some kind of behavioural dynamic that is made transparent across all users of the product in order to drive the required behaviour.

Single Twist	Behavioural Dynamic	Transparency Factor
Viral Effects	Selfish Rewards	Rewards accruing to individuals
	Altruism	Rewards accruing to others and to groups
Herd Behaviours	Information cascade	Decision making in real time
	Path dependency	Historical decisions
Emergent Wisdom	Aggregation	New thinking behaviour
	Coordination	New physical behaviour

Table 6.3: Platform Features in a Single Twist

Let us start with the viral effects twist, which, as we know, is based on the idea that platform users can make themselves and their use of a product highly *observable*, and will do so if some kind of benefit accrues when they do so.

We also know there are two kinds of behaviours that drive this: firstly, when there is the possibility of selfish rewards when use of the product is made observable; and secondly, when there are altruistic rewards which accrue to groups using the product.

Each of these cases is slightly different. Consider again the examples of Amway and Twitter, both cases of viral effects twists based on selfish rewards. Amway is viral because individual sellers have a financial motivation to recruit other sellers. What is the thing that makes these new sellers join Amway? They see the financial rewards their sponsor – the person who is recruiting them into the network – is earning.

Actually, Amway is an example of a viral effects twist that's been taken to an extraordinary extreme: many of the most senior Amway distributors make most of their money not by selling Amway products and collecting royalties from their down-line, but through tickets to events and rallies where they pitch their personal success.

At Twitter, too, transparency of rewards is a key product feature. You can see how many followers each person has on Twitter very easily. But most particularly, having an elite Twitter account is an online measure of success unlike any other. If you have thousands of twitter followers you are someone, and there are hundreds of different sites that use Twitter follower counts to rank you competitively.

At the time of writing, the top three Twitter accounts in the world were, in order, Lady Gaga (the popstar), Justin Beiber (another pop star) and US President Barak Obama. Each had millions of followers. By contrast, I am the 44,000th most followed person on Twitter as of July 2011. Although the whole thing is an ego-trap, I have to admit I am as motivated as the next guy not to be so far down this league table, especially when getting to the top means I can be compared with Lady Gaga and the US President. (Perhaps I won't be in such a rush, however, if it means I must be compared to Justin Bieber, but that is besides the point.)

Viral twists can also be based on altruistic behaviour as well, of course, as demonstrated by the example of Kiva. The key product feature driving Kiva is its way of building in transparency of *group* benefits as a result of individual behaviour. This is done through the retelling of inspiring stories of life changes in the developing world. These, in turn, motivate further investment. Over time, Kiva investors increase their lending as they see the changes they, and their fellow investors, are making. In other words, consumption makes Kiva more compelling for everyone.

Herd behaviours twists work in a similar way; but instead of exposing rewards for individuals or groups, they make *decision making* transparent. It is this transparency which makes people herd together in the first place: they need a way to see what the crowd is doing so they can make a decision about what is *consistent with norms*, the key innovation attribute on which this twist is based.

Herd behaviours twists are transparent about either the decisions made by the majority of customers in the past, or about ones which are being made right now. In the former case, the twist sets up a path dependency. The decisions that users of the platform make now are dependent on the decisions the crowd has made in the past. Earlier, we looked at the fact that most people prefer the standard QWERTY keyboard layout, even though there are much more efficient alternatives available. Why don't people switch? Because they can see everyone has already made a decision to learn QWERTY.

The other kind of herd behaviours twist arises when you build features that make platform users' *current* decisions transparent. When people see what most other people are doing, they automatically prejudice their own decision making to work in the same way, creating an information cascade.

The various online product ratings systems, such as the ones featured on Amazon, are actually devices designed to induce information cascades. That's why products with reviews – particularly good ones – tend to sell well no matter how good they actually are. And we've already seen how offline information cascades can work: Treacy and Wiersema's book *The Discipline of Market Leaders,* became a best seller simply because the pair gamed the New York Time Best Seller list, which is a hugely visible information source consumed by millions.

Product features that cause information cascades are everywhere, of course. Having a restaurant that's full is no use at all in attracting more customers if people walking by can't see how full the restaurant is. It is the publically available prices of shares on exchanges that create bubbles and crashes, where the underlying value of companies is irrelevant to the buying or selling decision. Indeed, it was publically available information about the price of tulip bulbs in Amsterdam that led to the first ever market bubble, where monstrous prices were paid for flowers that lived for less than one week a year.

The underlying psychological dynamic behind all these behaviours is simple: though potential users may not have actual knowledge of the set of criteria that drove previous decisions, they can see the results of those decisions and infer some conclusions of their own. The herd behaviour develops when these inferences override any other objective data held by the decision maker.

What is the platform requirement for herd behaviour twists? The answer is simple: you create a system where the *outcomes* from everyone who's made a similar choice are available to those who are about to make the same choice.

The final kind of single twist is the *emergent wisdom twist,* and it too has two dynamics associated with it. The first dynamic arises as a result of information aggregation. The platform provides the circumstances where individuals are able to create new knowledge for themselves by experimentation of some kind. This new knowledge is then shared with everyone else and aggregated; the result is that the total knowledge on the platform is magnified for everyone.

I should pause here for a moment to characterise the difference between the platform features that make this kind of emergent wisdom twist different from the information cascade herd behaviour twist we just looked at.

In the latter case, individuals make their decisions based on *inference* from the results of the decisions of everyone else. They are usually not privy to the specific individual knowledge of those decision makers themselves and, indeed, their own specific knowledge gets overridden because they'd rather believe the crowd knows something they don't. If you're standing outside a crowded restaurant, and you conclude that it is therefore a good place to eat, the one thing you don't have access to is the feedback of everyone who's currently dining.

An emergent wisdom twist is quite different because it is the aggregation of all the local knowledge of individuals that makes the whole work. Individuals don't simply rely on the outcomes others have achieved; they examine the set of personal information that each decision maker had available.

Now, obviously, this is impossible as crowds grow larger, so a key platform feature that drives the emergent wisdom twist is some kind of aggregation facility. At CureTogether, the aggregation facility is statistical. You get statements similar to this: "1000 people have the common cold: 500 tried vitamin C, and 100 found it made a significant difference". The aggregation makes it possible to make a substantive judgement on the best possible decision for you based on the private information of everyone else. And when you record your outcomes, the total information available to everyone else improves too.

The second kind of emergent wisdom twist also uses trialability, but instead of creating knowledge, it coordinates action. In this case it is the actual behaviour of individuals using the platform which must be made transparent to make the twist work.

Another interesting website in this context is Geocaching.com, which is a platform supporting an outdoor sporting event of the same name. The site involves players equipped with GPS navigation systems follow clues on the website to various caches hidden at particular real world places. When they arrive at one of these destinations, they leave their code names and dates in a logbook to indicate they've successfully found the cache.

One of the parts of the game that's most interesting for our purposes is called a Travel Bug. A Travel Bug is an object attached to a unique tag with a serial number. Each Travel Bug has a mission, which is created by the person who sets it up. For example, a Travel Bug may have a goal of going to every continent on earth, and its progress is recorded step-by-step as Geocachers move it from cache to cache.

What does the Geocaching website do to coordinate its travel? The answer is nothing. But what the website does achieve is set up an emergent wisdom twist. The site has logs of where the Travel Bug has been, and descriptions of where it would like to go. Geocachers take the Travel Bug from cache to cache if they think it will help them with finding the next cache. There is often a lot of back-and-forwards, but in the great majority of cases, the Travel Bug *does* fulfil its mission. It is amazing to watch one as it meanders across the globe, tracked online, and without any coordination at all from the person who set it up in the first place.

DOUBLE TWIST DESIGN

Single twists make some kind of behavioural dynamic external to the actual product transparent in order to encourage platform users into the kinds of behaviour that reinforce the twist. The double twist, by contrast, is much simpler: it relies on *exposing* the price/performance curve to users. This is done in different ways depending on the kind of double twist being implemented, as summarised in Table 6.5:

Double Twist Type	Behavioural Dynamic	Product Features
Direct product improvement	More useful as more people use it	Transparency between customers
Ecosystem improvement	More useful as more complimentary products are produced	Transparency of Ecosystem Transparency between customers
Locality improvement	More useful with social or geographic proximity	Transparency of local linkages Transparency between customers

Table 6.5: Platform Features in a Double Twist

Let us first turn our attention to the simplest case of a double twist, that where product price/performance directly improves with consumption. What makes these twists work, in practice? Twists based on direct network effects are dependent on some way for customer groups to see each other using the product.

Let us consider some of the examples we've been looking at in this book, starting with the telephone. In this case, there are two customers groups – those making calls and those receiving them. Both can obviously observe the other using the phone, since they are talking to each other. Here, the transparency is provided by various mechanisms that permit both groups to see how many other people they can call, which is the function of telephone directories, both paper and online.

What about men and women on dating sites and in nightclubs? Both the live venue and the website are again platforms which improve with consumption, because no one goes to either when there aren't lots of other people already there. The important thing about nightclubs and dating sites, however, is both men and women can see how each group are using the platform, at both an individual and collective level. Transparency in a nightclub is provided by the very visible mating ritual that goes on between prospective couples, which starts with furtive glances across the room, and ends with gyrations on the dance floor. All of this is visible to everyone else in the nightclub.

On a dating site, there may not be furtive glances and dance floor gyrations, but sensible platform operators provide alternatives for each stage of the courting process. On some sites, for example, you can send a "wink" – a digital message that lets a prospect know you're looking at their profile. This is the functional equivalent to the furtive glance in the real world scenario of a nightclub.

Wikipedia, a double twist-driven effort to make an encyclopaedia of the world's knowledge, is no different. Again, there are two groups of customers: contributors and readers. And, again, each can see what the other does in great detail. One day, I woke up to discover I have a profile on Wikipedia. I don't know who created it nor their motivation for doing so, but the interesting thing was watching readers and contributors discuss what was appropriate, or not, to put in it. The transparency of the comments page behind every Wikipedia entry is what enables this collaboration to occur.

As I mentioned earlier, however, collaboration and transparency are not always the ready bedfellows of all classes of product. They lend themselves excellently to categories that are steeped in social interaction, but are much less applicable to those that are consumed in splendid isolation, like banking and other financial services. Or are they?

I used to think banking was a product category that would *never* be subject to a double twist. Consider what would have to change for a double twist to operate successfully. Firstly, you'd have to find a group of customers in a bank willing to share their details, and a bank willing to let them. Secondly, returns to each customer group would need to improve as consumption of banking services increased.

Since it was banks that ran the world's economy into the ground trying to ensure any benefits resulting from increased consumption accrued to them alone (that was the function of the sub-prime market, by the way), such a scenario seemed, to me, to be remote at best. But then, in the process of writing my last book *(Innovation and the Future Proof Bank)* I discovered a most unique institution.

It was an institution building a different way of doing banking in Spain, and though I didn't know it then, it was employing the double twist with extraordinary effectiveness. Caja Navarra is a Spanish savings bank with a difference. It contributes a percentage of its profits to charitable causes in the community, something all savings banks in Spain are required to do by law.

But instead of deciding which causes to support, it allows its customers to choose how their portion of its profits will be distributed. This sets up something highly unusual: there are two groups of customers at Caja Navarra, but they aren't borrowers and savers. Instead, the bank has charities and customers. Each collaborates with the other, and each finds the product improves with consumption.

For customers, as charities sign up at Caja Navarra, there are more charitable projects for them to choose from, so the benefits of having an account improve. And for charities, the more customers who switch to Caja Navarra, the better the financial returns they'll achieve through donations. Caja Navarra does something incredible from a transparency perspective: it actually *tells* its customers how much it makes from them. It also forces charities to tell customers what they do with their money at an individual level.

It will not surprise anyone reading this book that this double twist has propelled the institution to the very top of the league table in Spain, so much so that recently, they announced the formation of Caja Civica, a new bank based on the merger of three savings banks, including Caja Navarra.

So, as it turns out, any product category can be part of a double twist, so long as transparency between customer groups enables increasing value with increasing consumption.

If direct observation between customer groups is the way to drive a product double twist, what is needed to create a twist based on an ecosystem? As before, the product must still have features to enhance transparency between customers, but this time, it is also necessary to make sure that complimentary products are transparent too.

Let us again consider some of the examples we've looked at in this book. Apple's App Store achieves ecosystem transparency with the iPhone by providing a special software application – the App Store itself – that showcases every application available. As you can see from Figure 5.2 (page 145), the introduction of this ecosystem double twist had a substantial impact on the fortunes of the device, kick-starting it to a sales level it probably would not have achieved without.

In the App Store, Apple go to great lengths to make sure consumers have a good view of its expanding ecosystem. There are category "top picks" pages, where Apple staff select for special prominence an application they think will sell. There are best-sellers lists and most-popular lists, and even a feature called "Genius", which looks at the applications you've previously bought, and makes recommendations for others you might like based on several different factors.

Of course, if all customers had was a shopping catalogue of new bits of functionality for installation, App Store would probably not be as effective as it has proven. The difference is App Store also allows customers to see how other customers are using their phones. It does this through the provision of rating and comment features. After a certain number of uses, customers are often asked to provide a rating for an application, expressed as a number of stars. Optionally, customers can also write a review. These details, in aggregated format, are presented along with the application in App Store, so customers can not only see the ecosystem, they can evaluate how everyone else is using it.

For another example of a double twist based on ecosystems, we can also look at Facebook, whose killer blow to rival MySpace was competing on the basis of having most things you could do with your social network, rather than having the most content available *for* a social network. Here, too, the preconditions for a decent ecosystem double twist are evident. In particular, it is the fact that every single person connected to you on Facebook is told you've installed a complimentary product (by way of the News Feed) that drives the ecosystem double twist.

Of course, Facebook is primarily an example of a locality double twist, to which an ecosystem twist was added later. Facebook's locality double twist is based on the fact that the links between individuals are personal, and therefore valuable. This is what sets it apart from other social networks, such as MySpace and even Twitter, whose viral single twist makes it desirable to sign up as many people as possible, whether they are known to each other or not.

Because each link on Facebook is important to those making them, with increasing consumption (i.e., more links are added) the product improves. Facebook's personal links generates an important additional feature: once you've linked to a friend, you're able to see *their* personal links, too. Each linkage, therefore, expands your locality exponentially.

NEXT UP

The focus of this chapter was to explore some of the issues product planners are likely to encounter when trying to create a sidestep and twist for themselves. Primarily, these deal with specific features needed in a platform to make twists work, and the mechanics of creating sidesteps which support on-going improvement of the price/performance curve.

However, these specific theoretical discussions provide limited insight about how to make the sidestep and twist work for product features. For a more complete understanding, it is also necessary to examine the organisational and strategic context of companies considering implementing this strategy. It is this key topic to which we'll turn our attention in the final chapter of *Sidestep &Twist*.

STRATEGIC
RECOMMENDATIONS

CHAPTER SEVEN

When I first started talking in public about the ideas expressed in *Sidestep & Twist,* I was startled by the fact that so many people responded in one of two ways. Some came up to me and indicated they were relieved I'd suggested breakthroughs might be less a driver of value than organisations have traditionally believed. They were people with stories. I was told of innovation teams going wild, creating new things that customerS didn't want and couldn't afford.

Some people were even more forthright. They explained that their organisations had invested millions in programmes for which they'd done much customer research in advance. They'd explored every option from every angle, and made a *rational* business decision to create a breakthrough. Yet, even with all that careful preparation, they still didn't achieve market success. One person even said to me: "Not all innovation is good innovation", a line which I have consistently used to describe the sidestep and twist ever since.

There were also those who took quite the opposite view. They were nervous I was proposing that creativity, insight and taking risks was inappropriate in large organisations, and following such a line to its conclusion would result in round after round of derivative businesses, all recycling the same thing. They, too, were people with stories.

The theme that emerged most often was how the "bean counters", or the "operators", or any of the other detail-oriented disciplines, had crushed the life out of companies. They were stories of devastation of talent and the ultimate elimination of all that was exciting and decent in a company when it started. The point, they told me, was that creativity and innovation are primary drivers of value, and therefore, should be celebrated rather than discouraged. There is merit in both these views, of course. What is more important, however, is that it is quite likely both views will exist in any given organisation. This, perhaps, is the greatest challenge for anyone considering how the sidestep and twist might be useful to *them*.

But there are other things to consider, too. Therefore, in what remains of this book I'll present seven recommendations for companies considering an application of the sidestep and twist, based on the observations I've made from firms I've studied while preparing this material. Then, finally, I'll summarise this book chapter by chapter, pulling out the key points from each for reference.

Before we proceed, I'd like to share one last story of a firm that's had success employing the sidestep and twist. That firm is Spigit, a Californian company that makes tools to support innovation management in large enterprises.

A CORPORATE SIDESTEP AND TWIST

In 2011, I left my secure, well paid, job-for-practically-life as Chief Technology Officer in one of Britain's biggest government departments after just two years of service. I did it because I was fascinated by something a unique company called Spigit was doing: building crowds of people who would work synergistically together to make their organisations better.

What was so fascinating about a small internet start-up in Silicon Valley? The answer is they'd built a product, one using all the mechanics of the sidestep and twist.

Let me start by explaining what Spigit does, and how their method is a sidestep from what went before. Companies using Spigit seem, on the surface, to have implemented little more than a corporate suggestion box. You know the type of thing I mean: a place in which you can put your ideas for someone else to action. Suggestion boxes have been around for hundreds of years. There are actually records of them being used in Victorian times, where they were little wooden post boxes into which slips of paper could be inserted by anyone who had anything to say.

The problem with these schemes is they usually don't work. Sometimes they *seem* to be a success, if you define that term by how many pieces of paper get submitted. But the problem is what to do with all the pieces of paper once you have them? If you get too many, providing responses quickly becomes a bigger effort than seems justified for the kinds of suggestions being made. On the other hand, if you get no suggestions at all, the scheme is a failure anyway.

The advent of computer suggestion boxes changed things a bit, and were the first sidesteps from the physical post boxes that had been around for many years. They improved things by allowing everyone to see what contributions everyone else had made, and in some cases they allowed crowds to vote on the ideas they liked the best.

That was the state of the industry before Spigit came along. The sidestep Spigit introduced used the power of crowds in a much deeper way than what had gone before. And it was not before time, either. The fact is, most innovation programmes are cancelled in 18 months or less, and the reason is they don't achieve very much. Having led several, I know this from personal experience. Doing innovation in large corporations is hard, probably more difficult even than being responsible for a large corporate transformation or reorganisation. What makes the innovation problem so challenging? The answer has two parts.

Firstly, the role of an innovator is bringing new things to the market, but as we've seen in this book, brand new things are slow to take off. Initially, only a few, very few customers are interested because of the risks involved. Since customers are risk averse, they need to be told something works by people they trust. Then, too, if something is *that* brand new – perhaps even a breakthrough – it may be too expensive in terms of price/performance to be all that interesting to anyone.

It takes time before these issues get sorted out, either by repeated sidesteps, or because subsidies and/or bundling have stimulated the market artificially. Meanwhile, the main business lines of a typical organisation may have been running for years. They'll have established revenues and systems and processes; and they'll have large numbers of customers, and lots of employees to serve them.

Compared to any new product introductions, the mainline business has all the advantages, and the poor innovators have a really tough time justifying their existence. Often, when the balance of investment to returns is examined in any detail, brand new innovations look like a very poor decision indeed.

The other reason doing innovation in large corporations is difficult is this: if a new product is successful, particularly if it is a sidestep from the existing business, it can be seen as a threat by those who control the old business. So if you're a corporate innovator, you're likely to face an uphill battle. Very, very few teams succeed.

Spigit changed that, and it did it by adding a very unique double twist, where an organisation's innovation capability grows as more innovation occurs. As that happens, the challenges I've just outlined become less significant.

How did Spigit achieve this? Basically, it changed the paradigm for innovation from centralised command and control – where the innovators sit in a corporate centre and have to push out their creations to a less than adoring world – to a social one. Or, stated in another way, Spigit makes it possible for people at the edge of organisations, those closest to customers, to do innovation themselves by making their interactions transparent.

Spigit is an organisation that creates crowds at the edge of organisations, and then uses various twists to motivate them to get things done. Crowds, when they've been built, are very powerful instruments. Most people imagine they're useful because they provide you with hundreds, perhaps thousands, of pairs of eyes and ears, and you can use them to spot opportunities to make improvements.

That's what old-style innovation management platforms do, of course: provide organisations with suggestions for things that can be done differently. You still have to find a way to make things happen, and since that is done in the context of the challenges for innovators I outlined a moment ago, even when you have a large-sized crowd thinking about innovation, you're by no means guaranteed a successful innovation.

Spigit enables crowds to use their thousands of pairs of hands, too. Here's how. Firstly, anyone in an organisation that has Spigit can enter their ideas for change, in much the same way as any other kind of idea management platform. That's where the similarities end, however, because for each idea entered, you get a wage, expressed in a virtual currency. You also get wages for voting, commenting and rating ideas, and the balance of every individual in the system is transparent to everyone else. As you'd expect, this sets up an interesting competition between people to see who can be the richest.

If that was all people could do to earn virtual currency, things would get boring quickly. But Spigit is clever in the way it motivates people to do things. Ideas can be voted on certainly, but even if they have lots of votes they're unlikely to go very far unless a few other conditions have been satisfied.

For starters, you generally have to get a significant number of people interested in your idea – measured by how much activity they're contributing to its development. If you fail to do so, no matter how clever the suggestion, it tends get buried at the bottom of the pile. Ideas at the bottom of the pile usually die a quick death, since people are unlikely to see them at all. Interest wanes. And they get automatically deleted because they're going nowhere.

If you are able to get enough crowd activity, the idea might "graduate" to an internal stock market, where you can use your virtual currency to buy and sell shares in the ideas you like the most. Now, if an idea actually gets implemented, and you have shares in it, you get a virtual currency payoff. And, of course, if something goes wrong and it *doesn't* get implemented, you lose what you've invested altogether.

Something interesting happens when people have to invest their own virtual currency in an idea. Suddenly, they care a great deal about its future. They go so far as to spend their own time working on it. In some organisations, teams of people work on ideas, and selectively release information about their progress to affect the price. Yes, they effectively engage in insider trading in virtual currency. The whole thing is surprisingly amusing and addictive. You can imagine the dynamics all this sets up, since they're based entirely on the twists we've been discussing in this book.

Spigit uses twists to encourage this behaviour in a number of ways. Overarching Spigit is a locality double twist that's practically the same as the one Facebook uses for social interaction, except in Spigit, people form connections around *ideas* they care about. These connections are valuable, since they are local to those who care about changing their organisations in one specific way. People are surprisingly passionate about their own ideas, it turns

out. This passion tends to manifest itself as a viral effects twist
based on an altruistic motivation. The group knows it needs to
make sure as many people as possible contribute to the idea if it
is to progress. So they use various tools in the platform to ensure
others vote positively, contribute reviews and do other things
which move it forward. The viral effects twist is working because
the *group* gets the reward if the idea is moved forward, and to do
that it must be seen by as many people as possible.

Once an idea is popular enough to list on the idea market,
what happens next is the result of a herd behaviours twist.
People tend to invest their virtual currency in ideas whose price
is rising. Their objective in doing so is to make a speculative gain
if the idea goes live. So Spigit implements a herd behaviour twist
using an information cascade. Everyone tends to buy into ideas
they believe will succeed, but the signals they use to determine
if that's likely to happen are the buying behaviours of everyone
else around them.

Such buying behaviour has an interesting effect. When you
ask individuals to vote on ideas, the intent that's expressed is "I
like this". But when you ask them to *buy* into an idea, the intent
that's expressed is, instead, "I believe in this". Users of Spigit
tend to part with their hard-earned currency *only* for ideas they
strongly believe in. Often, the belief is strong enough that they
join the group that proposed the idea in the first place. Over
time, the most successful ideas tend to form very large groups
who are all socially connected to each other, *and* who have a
vested interest in making their idea turn into reality.

This is a very, very powerful set of social dynamics, and one
which I got to see first hand, since I was part of the team that
implemented Spigit in UK government departments. In the
department I was a part of, a study by analysts[14] found we'd

---

14   "Case Study: Innovation Squared – The Department
for Work and Pensions turns Innovation into a Game." Gartner
(November 2010).

saved £21 million in hard cash, all because of the sidestep and twist we'd implemented with Spigit's help.

What is the number one thing I learned from this experience? I have to say it is this: the sidestep and twist can work, but the effort in getting it to do so can be significant. The work comes not from the difficulty in designing products and services that can use the concept, but trying to convince an established organisation that following such a course is a good idea.

So, with these thoughts in mind, below are the collection of strategic considerations I promised earlier.

NO. 1: CREATIVITY IS NOT ENOUGH TO BE SUCCESSFUL

Professionally, I've spent years working in various companies trying to "do" innovation. And, for years, I used to tell people we were "looking for the next big thing", or "finding a spark of genius", or something similar. It wasn't until I began to examine why so many of my efforts were failing that I began to understand why this was the wrong approach.

As we've seen elsewhere in this book, really genuine newness is actually very expensive for customers. Typically, it has a price/performance curve sufficiently poor that most of the people you want to convince to adopt it won't be able to do so. And the implication of *that* is you won't make much money. However, I had to learn this the hard way, by failing, and by getting fired for failing.

It wasn't that the things my teams and I were working on were bad, *per se*, but they were new enough that there weren't enough people willing to take a chance on them to become commercially viable. At least, not in the timeframe available.

The link between creativity and profits is a myth that's been repeated so many times it seems its almost been accepted as a "corporate truth". Consequently, the kinds of people who routinely fill our product development teams are those bursting with ideas and sparkling with vision. There is, however, nothing more dangerous to the longterm viability of a product development programme. Creatives, being driven by the joy of doing genuinely new stuff, are rarely satisfied with repurposing what has gone before in order to achieve incremental improvements in price/performance for an existing category.

They always seek to create brand new categories, since this optimises their personal sense of satisfaction. In the short term, too, it is likely to gain them significant kudos as executives applaud their creation of something competitors don't have. However, the applause seems to die quite quickly when the new stuff fails to sell rapidly enough to justify the investment. Because critical mass occurs at the intersection of price/performance and adoption S-curves, even if there is genuine demand for the new category, it takes much longer than anyone expects for it to become profitable.

If history is anything to go by, a new innovation will usually require much significant additional investment in terms of sidesteps before it *does* become profitable. Your creatives *might* strike it lucky and build something that takes off all by itself, but personally, I have been unable to find a single example of that occurring in all my research. Not a single example, actually, which didn't have one or more sidesteps before it achieved commercial success.

Are there *any* circumstances where it makes sense for a truly breakthrough product to be brought to the market? Well, yes. The first of these is where it is possible to accelerate the price/performance curve to ensure there are enough people who can afford the product so critical mass is possible. This is the effect of the bundle, or subsidy, we examined in Figure 6.2 (see page 168): by adding new functionality or dropping the price, adoption can happen at a much faster rate than would occur otherwise. In other words, you can artificially get the effect of multiple sidesteps in a very short period of time.

The other circumstance in which a breakthrough product can succeed is where conditions make it possible to buy enough adopters that critical mass can be achieved *without* waiting for the price/performance to improve to a stage that justifies mass adoption at the critical mass point. Buying adopters is quite different to a subsidy or bundle. It is different because what one seeks to do is acquire, artificially, enough of the innovator segment to advance the curve to point A (see Figure 2.1, page 46).

Following that, the objective is next to acquire enough of the early adopter segment to get the curve to point B. To actually do this requires delivering offers targeted at very, very specific sub-segments of a total market. These offers need to be designed to move adoption along *regardless* of whether it would ordinarily make sense for those individuals to adopt if they only considered price/performance.

A subsidy or bundle, on the other hand, targets the whole market indiscriminately. Either way, the key issue is working out *how* you'd target these key segments to move the adoption curve forward. Who *are* those people anyway? Even if you *could* find out, how much effort can a marketing team really afford to spend on each one to convince them to adopt?

These are challenging questions, which are usually pretty difficult to answer. I mean, if it were easy why would any company do mass media advertising in the first place? Targeted marketing is obviously much more effective.

So, if it is possible to manipulate price/performance or the adoption S-curve, then it may make sense to allow the creatives to pursue a breakthrough. The challenge, often, is that the creatives come up with the breakthrough *before* the decision has been made to do the massive spend necessary to artificially prop it up in the market.

So my advice is this: watch the creatives! Be very sure that if you're going to let them do something unique, you've got the financial wherewithal to support the whole market for however long the category takes to mature. Or, be sure you're willing to buy enough of the market that it doesn't matter whether it is mature or not. For most companies, both options are too expensive to take on routinely.

NO. 2: PAY ATTENTION TO PRICE/ PERFORMANCE

This discussion on the dangers of unbridled creativity in product development raises other issues. If you examine the processes people follow when they prepare a case for a new product, much of the time is spent on forecasting of unit sales. If a product actually is successful in the market, it is likely sales will follow an S-shaped adoption curve of the kind we saw in Figure 2.1 (see page 46).

Adoption curves have taken innovation theorists a long way towards understanding why some products are successful and others are not. Failed products, they argue, don't get to critical mass for whatever reason, and therefore were doomed from the start.

The problem with this argument, of course, is that it implies if you *can* get a product to critical mass point, you'll win. This leads to a belief that comprehensive marketing should be enough to make any new product a substantive success. Now, if that were true, some of the biggest product flops of all time should not have happened. The Segway transporter, for example, had enough marketing hype behind it that it should easily have penetrated the critical innovator and early adopter segments. Yet it failed in the market. Why?

The answer is that by looking only at adoption S-curves, your focus is directed towards the demand side of the market without understanding the supply side. There is no point having a brilliant, first-of innovation if it is too expensive for anyone to actually buy or too complicated for anyone to understand. This is where the price/performance curve comes in. Figure 2.2 (page 57) shows how these two curve interact.

As we've seen already, critical mass usually happens at the intersection between price/performance and the S-curve, because that's when the right number of people can afford to use the product to drive critical mass in the first place. Before that, multiple sidesteps are usually required in order to make a breakthrough good enough and cheap enough for customers to actually buy.

What this means for product planners is difficult choices must be made, and sometimes, they must be made without very much data to back them up. One option is to wait until the price/performance measure is sufficiently good that enough adopters are in a position to use the product. This is a strategy that works in the medium and long terms, especially where there is little possibility that competitors will show up.

However, for most product development teams, waiting is a poor option that endears them neither to their managers or the financial controllers of their companies. Management always gets nervous when they're asked to believe in something without early results, particularly when the product is more of a breakthrough than they're used to.

Two choices remain: either bring the price down in order to make the product less risky to those in the first adoption segments; or, add performance so the risk is worth it.

The former case is straightforward: you simply find a way to buy adoption until critical mass is achieved. The latter, though, is more difficult to achieve, as most companies have to choose: they either build more capability as quickly as possible, or bundle existing capability in. Both are potentially unattractive as they add cost.

In the end, the dilemma remains: either wait for returns, or pay up to accelerate them. You can see why, for most organisations and corporate innovators, developing products that are genuinely new is economically a risky proposition!

NO. 3: YOUR PLAN CANNOT BE: "BUILD IT AND THEY WILL COME"

Having just suggested that "waiting for returns" is a sensible strategy, it is important to point out I'm not suggesting all the work ends the moment a product hits the market. Time and time again, I have seen organisations do something which is guaranteed to fail: they create a product or service which is brilliant, and think brilliance is enough for the product to be widely accepted.

In fact, I have done this myself. My first deployment of Spigit, which was in a major bank, was like this. I was so caught up with all the amazing features of the tool I just assumed a crowd would form all by itself. I learned this was something of a fantasy. The reality is, no matter how amazing the product, very few people are willing to try something new without positive reinforcement from people they trust. In fact, the only people who are willing to try anything genuinely new are the innovators – those who are so risk friendly they don't care if things go wrong and they're personally put out by the failure.

When we first looked at adoption S-curves in Chapter 3, we saw how the innovator segment comprises 2.5% or less of any market. This is why "build it and they will come" is usually a failing strategy: the only people who will come are the innovators, and at the start there are too few of them to make any difference. What's really needed is the *early adopter* segment – a much more healthy 13.5% or so of the market. Of course, they're unlikely to adopt unless you've reached a significant percentage of the innovators.

Herein lies the significant challenge. Who are the innovators? How can you reach them even if you can identify them in the first place? For most companies and most products, this challenge is sufficiently great that there's little choice but to fall back on mass-media marketing methods. By targeting the whole market with messages, the chances of getting to the innovator and early adopter segment is high; but of course, this is probably the most expensive possible approach.

One of the key insights that led me to want to write this book came when I noticed the adoption decision for most people is not a binary-type calculation, as most innovation theorists have suggested in their adoption models. People *will* accept more risk that a brand new product won't work well for them if the price is less, or if the performance appears to be better. Hence, the number of innovators and early adopters *increases* if the price/performance of a new product improves. This is the mechanism that drives the equilibrium point of Figure 2.2 (see page 57).

How can you improve price/performance to get more innovators and early adopters? Throughout this book, I've suggested that the most effective strategy is to wait for the incremental improvement you get from repeated sidesteps over time. That's not realistic, of course, for products that need to be successful in a short time period, particularly when the product is already in the "race to recruit" phase (see Figure 6.2, page 168).

Then, you have little choice but to consider subsidies or bundling. It is always quite a surprise to me to discover companies who launch new products without making plans to get the initial group of adopters on board. Since my move from the government sector to Spigit, I have had the chance to observe this for real on so many occasions.

There is a marked difference between the innovation performance of companies that actively recruit crowds into the process and those that don't. Some, repeating the mistake I made myself in my first deployment, imagine the *functionality* of the platform is all that is needed to create enough interest. Usually, what happens is there is a flurry of interest triggered by whatever initial marketing accompanies the launch. Then, such crowds as exists go somewhere else.

On the other hand, some organisations go out of their way to identify their innovative players and take specific steps to make sure they're engaged. What happens then? The innovators take over the recruitment process and recruit the early adopters and other segments all by themselves. Those are the organisations that have the most success, of course.

NO. 4: EVERYTHING CAN BE TWISTED

One of the reasons companies think, "Build it and they will come" works is they've added a twist to their product without knowing it. In these cases, quite in spite of themselves, they achieve success without really knowing why. Unfortunately, many companies develop the twist part of their proposition relatively late in the process. This is understandable. In the rush to get a product out the door so the initial R&D investment can be recovered, it seems sensible to concentrate on building features that might attract more customers. In fact, this is a reasonable strategy, since adding features enhances the price/performance curve. This, in turn, makes it *economic* for more people to adopt the product.

A focus on features may be a good strategy at the beginning of a product's life. However, there is a danger involved in allowing feature production to dominate strategically. The danger is that early successes with features can lead companies to believing a twist is unnecessary. There are few cases where features alone are much use in sustaining long term competitive advantage, no matter how good they are. Sooner or later, someone else will do the same sidestep. Perhaps many will do so.

When lots of people enter a market with the same product, all one needs is an understanding of the most basic economics to predict the outcome: commoditisation. The most commonly employed response to this problem is to block entrants by obtaining legal protections to restrict supply of key inputs, like copyrights and patents. Another is to establish a twist, and to do it as early as possible.

Sometime, though, it isn't *obvious* that a twist is available, or even that one is possible. In 2011, I was presenting the material in *Sidestep & Twist* at a financial services conference in Australia. After giving my presentation, an attendee said, "Yes, interesting, but how does all this apply to financial services?" Unfortunately, my preparation was obviously poor, because I did not have an effective answer to hand. I rather suspect that, as a result, my content was less well received than it could have been.

The experience, however, was valuable, because it forced me to think about the sidestep and twist in the context of organisations beyond the ones I was researching for this book. When I was forced to do that, I realised *every* market has all the qualities required to support a twist, just as every market is made up of products which have been derived from multiple sidesteps.

For example, every single market I can think of has multiple, independent customer groups. Banking, for instance, has borrowers and savers. Pension funds have workers and retirees. Capital markets have investors and investees. Look hard enough and you can find multiple dependent customer groups everywhere.

The second quality needed for a successful twist is the ability to generate value with increased consumption; and it is this value that enables a company to charge a price. Here, I had to think hard. The financial services industry – one of the most commoditised in existence – has historically had something of a love affair with intellectual property protections, particularly patents. They've used them to lock out competitors who, lets face it, don't have to do much to replicate any competitive advantage someone dreams up in the industry.

But what kind of financial services products can you imagine where *consumption* makes the product better? And who in the financial services industry would be open to such products? Practically speaking, you don't have to look far for ideas as to what is *possible*. Zopa, a peer-to-peer lending site in the UK, has built a product connecting borrowers and savers without the intermediary of a bank. The key feature is both sides benefit as more people join. The value improves with consumption, in this case, because there are more opportunities for both to save and lend.

Kiva, an organisation we've looked at earlier, is another example. They make loans to the developing world based on how observable both lenders and borrowers are: as more of both groups have success, it makes others more interested in joining the service as well. What is common amongst these financial services products, and indeed amongst *all* products that use a twist, is they are based on making the actions of consumers transparent to all other users of the same product.

Returning to the retelling of my experience at this Australian conference, I decided to test how open financial institutions might be to creating products with features that enhance transparency between customers. I suggested to a pension planner that it would be interesting to create a product where an emergent wisdom twist might allow the crowd to determine specific investment choices for the whole fund, perhaps with an aggregation mechanism based on voting.

Then I proposed the performance of the fund over all, and the course chosen by the crowd, be compared with the performance the fund *would* have achieved if the individual investor's options had been chosen. This information would be available to everyone. Finally, I suggested the choices of those who over-performed compared to the crowd be given greater weight in *subsequent* investment decisions.

Now, this was only a hypothetical product, but my suggestion was met with something only little short of horror. How, this planner wanted to know, could a crowd of untrained individuals *possibly* do better than professionals with their market data tools and financial models and statistics? And, he went on, what sorts of customers would ever *dream* of sharing such personal financial information anyway? To answer this latter point, I explained the workings of CureTogether, a site sharing information even more personal and confidential than individual financial data. Though still doubtful, the planner had to concede that some people at least would likely share.

But his first point was much more difficult to answer. How can you tell a professional with almost 40 years experience that his skills could be replicated by crowds with no professional experience at all? The fact is, you have to see an emergent wisdom twist in action before you really believe one can work. My pension planner was still coming to grips with the internet, so the concept of crowds of connected people chatting and collaborating on matters that, traditionally, have been considered very private was more than a little alien. This is a typical response from any person who has been in a traditional business for a long time. Brought up with notions of value based on scarcity, they are challenged in the extreme when confronted with a business where value develops only with consumption.

If it is possible to find twists even in financial services, it must surely be possible to do it everywhere simply by working out how to make product usage between customers transparent. This leads me to the primary reason many organisations believe their products and services can't be twisted: they do not see how their current products and services can be transparency-enabled.

NO. 5: WATCH THE LAGGARDS

This discussion takes us to an important point, one of significance to anyone proposing a sidestep and twist in any large organisation. That point is this: a significant percentage of individuals will simply not accept a strategy can be successful that relies on: a) copying something that is already working; and b) then trying to give away as much of the product as possible.

How significant a percentage will be disbelievers? For an answer, we return again to the classification of adopters we first examined in Chapter 2. From our discussion there, we know there's a graduation of preferences for new ideas, ranging from innovators, who will adopt everything immediately no matter how risky, to laggards who'll adopt nothing unless they're forced to do so.

The central idea of the sidestep and twist is subject to exactly the same conditions. With that in mind, referring to Figure 2.1 (see page 46), we can make some statements about how difficult it will be getting a sidestep and twist adopted.

Firstly, laggards, which will be at least 16% of decision makers in an organisation, are a lost cause. They'll need to be forced into agreement by majority consensus. They're so completely risk averse they'll always prefer what's working today, no matter how good the arguments for change.

Early and late majority are also not much use, because though they're more open to innovation than the laggards, they're sufficiently risk averse that they'll avoid doing something as different as the sidestep and twist without plenty of evidence. That group makes up 68% of the decision makers in an organisation, and they'll be sitting on the fence, undecided, until something is done to convince them.

To do the convincing, all that remains is the 16% of management who are open and interested in brand new things. These key managers are probably not sufficient themselves to make a positive decision (unless one of them is the CEO – a rare and fortunate occurrence), but what they *can* do is convince the others. However, my experience suggests to me it is simply not enough to convince the leading 16% of management to be successful.

The reason is laggards are a powerful group. They will not sit on the fence silently when a major strategic change is proposed; they'll object vehemently. There is nothing malicious in this. Their behaviour is dictated by an innate caution and care, which makes them ideal managers for businesses which are performing well and have always done so on the back of traditional and steady revenue streams. In fact, it is quite likely the laggards in such businesses will have been promoted to the top because of these characteristics.

Recently, I spent some time working with an organisation whose core business was provision of technology services to large private sector companies. They had strict service level agreements with their customers, and were proud of the fact they rarely, if ever, missed them. In order to deliver to customers, they'd hired a group of experienced, steady managers who all knew exactly what kinds of risks needed to be eliminated in order to ensure their performance track record was unblemished. They'd hired, of course, a bunch of laggards, and in so doing had made sure that any and every change that could possibly affect them was systematically eliminated.

The problem is technology services of the kind they were providing were then – and still are – becoming commoditised. Having a great service record was just table stakes in the game they were playing. The real basis of competition was price. Their competitors, coming from lower-cost countries, had every advantage on that score. They were facing a really difficult decision: should they cut their costs and allow their service to suffer as a consequence? Or, would it be better to argue the value of their near-perfect performance and hope their customers would pay a premium? I proposed that the company try a sidestep and twist.

The proposition was, basically, that we'd implement a new online service management system (the sidestep), and couple that with an emergent wisdom twist (customers could trial solutions to their problems, with a statistical aggregation to see what worked most often).

Even in the face of price competition from competitors that was likely to have resulted in a complete loss of their business altogether, the laggards weren't willing to try it. Their arguments ranged from the sensible ("What about the risk if we let customers try things?") to the extreme ("Our customers aren't capable of helping themselves."). Their real objection, though, was none of the above. What they were really concerned about was trying something so completely *outside* their established experience. Laggards always react in this way when confronted with such a situation.

It is tempting to just ignore laggards and move on. This approach doesn't quite solve the problem, however: just as innovators and early adopters can convince the majority of a market to try something new, laggards are equally able to convince them *not* to try it. In this case, the laggards won out.

What would have needed to happen for my proposition to gain acceptance? In retrospect, I can see it would have been impossible to convince the laggard group to try the sidestep and twist, no matter what evidence I'd presented. Instead, I should have found a way to ensure their voices were balanced out by innovators and early adopters. Once again, one is in a race to recruit, which is a consistently recurring theme whenever a sidestep and twist is involved. In this case, it would have been a race to get more innovators and early adopters on board with the strategy *before* too many laggards found out about it.

Though it may be simplifying things somewhat, whenever you have more people supporting a sidestep and twist than laggards who are objecting to it, you'll likely be able to get the proposition adopted. The loudest group of voices always seems to win.

NO. 6: THE RACE TO RECRUIT

As I stated earlier, the race to recruit is a recurring theme in *Sidestep & Twist*. It is inevitable that whenever an easy sidestep is possible, the opportunity to do so will be taken up by a significant number of companies. If several of them are also employing a twist to lock out all these competitors, the winner is likely to be the organisation which reaches critical mass first, since that's the time when significant benefits from network effects begin to kick in.

After the critical mass point, consumption has the effect of making the over all product proposition better, so it becomes increasingly difficult for any competitor to get a grip on the market, and any competitors *already* in the market will either be forced to compete on price, subsidise adoption to counteract the twist, or exit altogether.

The race to recruit starts the moment a product is introduced. This race, as we saw earlier in Figure 6.2 (see page 168), involves reducing the price artificially by subsidies, or improving performance with bundling. This has to happen as quickly possible, because all other companies in the market will likely be doing the same thing.

The race to recruit has important implications for companies in crowded markets: spending money on new features and product enhancements at an early stage is not as good a strategy as using that investment to get more customers. The reason for this is quite simple: a subsidy or bundle has a more significant effect on price/performance than creating new functionality from scratch. Firstly, doing so takes time, and after all, this is a race to recruit.

But more importantly, subsidies and bundles are flexible, easily changed to optimise recruitment of customers. Product enhancements, on the other hand, aren't. They're laser-targeted at specific niches, and no matter how large the niche, are nonetheless a subset of the total market that can be addressed.

In a race to recruit, the key is being able to do whatever it takes to get as many customers as possible: *speed and flexibility* are the key drivers for success. Regrettably, it is often the case that companies fail to understand the urgency of this race to recruit. When they do so, the consequences are either expensive, at best; or result in the failure of the product altogether, at worst. The best rule of thumb is this: you cannot start twisting early enough.

NO. 7: TWISTS ARE NEVER EARLY ENOUGH

At Facebook, it was a combination of twists – a double twist based on localities, and a second one using an ecosystem of complimentary products – that eventually conquered MySpace. Facebook started to build the former the moment it launched, targeting an ultra-niche: college students at Ivy League schools. The timing is instructive because, ultimately, twist construction is actually a race to critical mass. In general – though not always – a company that achieves critical mass first will likely win any platform battle. And platform battles are a common occurrence whenever there is an easy sidestep to be made.

One of the most interesting battles for market supremacy at the moment is one we started to examine in Chapter 5 – that between Apple, Google and Microsoft for control of the new computing paradigm centred on smartphones.

The current position is as follows: Apple released iPhone, and later App Store, in late 2007. From Figure 5.2 (see page 145), we can see that critical mass for its platform occurred some time towards the end of 2008. Google announced its mobile phone operating system, Android, in November 2007, a few months behind the first version of iPhone. The first commercial handset using the software came out just under a year later, in October 2008, just before Apple reached critical mass with iPhone. By October 2010, the platform was the best-selling smartphone worldwide.

Meanwhile, Microsoft stagnated, losing market share to both iPhone and Android. By the time it finally responded with a brand new mobile phone platform of its own, Windows Phone 7, it was October 2010. It was way, way behind in terms of applications and users.

Each company has built its twists in different ways. Apple remains in a relatively strong position, since it still has (at time of writing) the most applications for its devices, something it achieved by building its twists earlier than anyone else. Android has always had to struggle to maintain parity in this area.

But Android achieved the greatest volume of sales by replicating a strategy that Microsoft had previously used to ensure Windows and MS-DOS was dominant: licence the operating system to anyone and everyone remotely interested in making mobile phones. The wide variety of handsets and manufacturers that produce Android phones has guaranteed that Google's operating system is one that has wide adoption. Android may not have the most apps, but it certainly has the most users.

So, in the platform battle, Apple has stitched up the developers, and Google has made sure it has the most users. This leaves Microsoft in a somewhat invidious position, with neither control of apps or users, something it needs in order to build a twist for itself. However, Microsoft is nothing if not canny when it comes to negotiating business arrangements for a new platform. In February of 2011, the company announced a partnership with Nokia. From now on, all Nokia smartphones would use Microsoft software. This relationship with the world's (then) largest manufacturer of cell phones has put Windows Phone 7 back in the game because Nokia's brand, distribution and existing user base are now all available to Microsoft.

But the company did not stop there. It then announced it was acquiring Skype, another company we've looked at briefly in these pages. Skype, you'll recall, is now the world's largest provider of long distance telephony, and is disrupting traditional telecommunications companies. How might Microsoft use these two arrangements to its advantage in a platform battle it otherwise seemed certain to lose?

Nokia users are loyal, dedicated to the brand and their choice of phone. In this respect, they share characteristics with Apple's own user base, a fact Apple used to its advantage when it first launched the iPhone. It is not inconceivable that a significant percentage of Nokia's large customer based will migrate to Windows 7 phones *en masse*. It would be a typical sidestep that follows the theoretical principals we've examined throughout this book: when you have a product that would otherwise have little adoption, if you can borrow the S-curve from somewhere else, you gain an artificial advantage.

So, the deal with Nokia speeds up adoption while through Skype Microsoft is able to adjust the price/performance aspect of its platform as well. Skype provides free long distance telephony to any other Skype user, and it has more users than any other similar platform. When Microsoft integrates Skype with its mobile phone, it will deliver a price point of zero for calls to a significant percentage of the long distance market.

It would be difficult for Apple or Google to match such a price/performance improvement, particularly if Microsoft restricts Skype use in the handsets of those companies. It is reasonable to suspect these two measures might kick start a twist, and bring Microsoft's platform to the critical mass point.

This scenario is, of course, largely conjecture. At the time of writing, it is not clear whether the Nokia relationship will bring Microsoft additional demand. Nor is it certain Skype will be integrated into Windows Phone 7.

What is clear, though, is faced with two dominant competitors, who both have twists past the critical mass point, Microsoft must build a twist of its own, or exit the mobile business a failure. Considering the history of the company at using twists successfully, *I* would not bet against it.

There is an important lesson we can learn from this platform battle: you can never start building your twist early enough. Both Apple and Google started theirs immediately. Microsoft, on the other hand, delayed. By the time it was ready to launch its handset, it had little choice but to *buy* itself a position in the market. Now, Microsoft has very deep pockets and can therefore afford to make a few strategic plays of this kind. Most companies, however, are not so lucky.

THE KEYS TO SIDESTEP AND TWIST

In these pages, we've gone to many different places. We've examined ways in which ideas spread, and how technologies supersede each other. We've explored the history of some of the most important technologies and businesses of our times. And we've looked at some pretty impressive failures as well, including some that at the time of writing are still in progress.

I would now like to condense all this material into a set of key points that should interest anyone considering implementing a sidestep and twist. What follows is a summary of those things, chapter by chapter, I found people were most interested in when I presented this material over the last year or so.

At the beginning of this book, in Chapter 1, we examined the story of John Ambrose Fleming, the creator of electronics. Fleming's breakthrough electronic valve has led to astounding changes in the world we lived in, yet he failed to gain any financial benefit from his invention. This story introduced us to the first key point of this book: breakthroughs, no matter how significant, rarely make their inventors much money.

On the other hand, organisations such as Google, who moved existing capabilities into new markets, as they have done with GPS navigation on their mobile phone handsets, have been very successful indeed. Their success is built on the concept of *sidesteps*.

In Chapter 2, we looked at the sidestep in detail. Sidesteps are driven by a simple economic reality: breakthroughs usually have poor price/performance characteristics when they're introduced. Consequently, most of the market will be too risk averse to adopt them. We examined why this was so by considering the rate at which individuals adopt new ideas: only 2% of a market is really open to genuine originality, and that's usually not enough to make an economic proposition work for anything that's cost very much to build. Yet, without that 2%, the rest of the market is unable to follow. This leaves companies in the difficult situation of either waiting for price/performance to improve (with later sidesteps), or taking artificial measures that reduce the risks of adoption sufficiently that the more risk averse parts of a market feel they can take a chance.

Whilst the supply side of the market is represented by price/performance, there is also a demand side, and it is governed by an adoption S-curve. This curve is driven by the way new ideas spread: initially, only the least risk averse are willing to adopt, but those individuals tell others of their experiences, which induce others to take up the product. The S-curve eventually reaches critical mass, at which point there is a rapid expansion of the product. S-curves and price/performance curves combine to give a total picture of the sidestep and twist and how it functions.

The other key point from this chapter was this: sidesteps are relatively easy to execute, so in any market where one is possible, it is likely there will be a lot of competition.

In Chapter 3, we examined a strategy for dealing with the likelihood of competition through the introduction of a twist. A twist arises in any situation where there are two or more customer groups and increased demand from one creates increased demand in the other. The other characteristic of a twist we examined is that where as consumption increases as a result of this demand, the over all attractiveness of the product improves as well.

These *network effects*, as they are known, have traditionally been thought to work only in situations where the product itself improves as consumption increases. But in our examination of the twist, we saw that network effects based on other innovation attributes could also arise. These attributes – consistency with norms, trialability and observability – are all aspects of the *single twist*.

In Chapter 4, we explored the single twist in detail. The single twist operates by speeding up the adoption S-curve as consumption expands. We saw how, when a twist incorporates trialability, you can build a platform that creates emergent wisdom, either because a crowd has discovered new things, or because they've coordinated to create new kinds of actions. When a twist incorporates consistency with accepted norms, the result is a platform where crowds exhibit herd behaviours – behaviours that reinforce the value of the product because everyone sees everyone else doing the same thing. And when you have a twist based on observability, you get viral expansion. In this latter case, customers recruit other customers, which makes the product more valuable.

Chapter 5 expanded on the *double twist,* the more conventional case of network effects where the product itself gets better with consumption. Double twists have the affect of speeding up adoption, and growing the market at the same time. The double twist also has three incarnations: the first, based on direct product improvement is the one with which most people are familiar. As consumption expands, the product becomes more capable: telephones and email are both examples of this at work.

The other two forms are somewhat less familiar. There are *ecosystem double twists,* where the core product doesn't improve with consumption, but additional complimentary products (often produced by third parties) arise, which help to improve the price/performance of the original. Apple was able to unseat its competitors in the smartphone market by offering a complete ecosystem, and Microsoft achieved several decades of monopoly over personal computing through the same approach.

The final kind of double twist is based on localities, either geographic or social. Here, value is generated with increased consumption, but it is value which is proportionate to the distance from the customer. Facebook, the example we examined in this chapter, won out over MySpace because the links between its customers were entirely personal: you had to know people well enough to email them before you could set up a link. MySpace links, by contrast, were little more than channels for broadcast, much the same way that Twitter followers work today.

By Chapter 6, the discussion had advanced to a consideration of the kinds of strategic questions confronting product planners considering adoption of a sidestep and twist approach. The answer to the key question – when to sidestep? – was, as often as possible. Of course, it is inevitable that eventually a company will run out of sidesteps and will face commoditisation as the price/performance curve levels out.

In response to this challenge, we next considered the twist, and the key considerations when building one. Whether it be a single or double twist, the conclusion was this: twists are really a race to achieve critical mass, or stated differently, a race to get as many customers as possible as early as possible.

In the final part of Chapter 6, the discussion moved onto the features needed to implement both single and double twists, and in both cases, the defining characteristic was this: transparency between customer groups drove the network effects to work.

Ultimately, although this book has covered a lot of ground, it is possible to summarise our conclusions in four simple statements:

1. Products that are already successful will likely continue to be so even if they're moved into other areas.

2. Breakthroughs, by contrast, usually take time to be successful, so their economics are challenging.

3. Once you have success, one way of preserving it is to do

things to lock your competitors out. Control of key knowledge
and other unique inputs is one way to do this.

4. However, a much better way is to build products that get
better the more they're used. If you get enough customers, you'll
have a product no one can unseat, no matter what.

THANK YOU AND GOODBYE

Let us return, finally, to the place this book started. In its opening pages, I made the assertion that one of the greatest myths of our time is breakthroughs can make you rich. If nothing else, I hope the arguments that followed have convinced you to take a hard look at any programs you're running in your organisations that are trying to create breakthroughs, especially if they're the ones you're betting your future on.

Though it may at times have seemed otherwise, the real point of this book was not to offer a case to eliminate creativity, innovation and genuine research as a corporate discipline. Rather, my intention was to show an alternative, more reliable, way to create the next generation of great products and services. These are products and services producers love because they are much less risky and expensive. And loved also by customers, because they get better the more they use them.

With these thoughts in hand, then, all that remains is to thank you for reading *Sidestep & Twist*. As an author, it is humbling to know how much personal time you gave to reach this page, and I hope you find your investment repaid many times over.

AFTERWORD

A few months after I completed the manuscript for this book, I woke one morning to the discovery that Steve Jobs, chief executive at Apple Computer had died after a protracted fight with cancer.

His death happened just a few days after his company released its next iteration of iPhone, a device ushering in a new core feature: deeply integrated voice control. You may recall during our discussions of herd behaviour twists, I suggested the only thing that might conceivably displace traditional keyboard data entry was speech interfaces, and lo-and-behold, Apple have added it to the one product where keyboards have traditionally been problematic.

Siri, as the new feature is known, is comprehensive, and though it has been on the market for only a few days at the time I wrote this afterword, reviews seem to indicate that it may, indeed, be a replacement for the keyboard that the world has been waiting for – at least on smartphones.

I am certain that Steve, had he lived just a while longer, would have been leading from the front as his company tackled speech – the next great human interface advancement for computing – just as he was at the beginning with graphical user interfaces, and then later with touch interfaces as implemented in the phenomenally successful iPhone and iPad.

In the time between completing this manuscript and its publication, other events of interest to readers have occurred too.

Firstly, according to Comscore data in October 2011, the fortunes of Windows Phone 7 seem to be improving. Until this point, Microsoft's phone platform was haemorrhaging users; October was the first month new users joining the Microsoft phone platform exceeded those leaving. It is a metric which bodes particularly well for Microsoft; one that is entirely consistent with its previous track record in buying demand for its platform. As I mentioned earlier in the book, I for one, would not bet against the company when it focuses on its core competence of pushing products – regardless of technology superiority – through their critical mass points.

Another development which may be of interest to readers is the latest set of features to have come from Facebook. Having built itself a business on a locality double twist, it seems the company has recognised it has now created a situation where all that information being spread down the personal links between its customers has gotten out of control. It has, consequently, redesigned this feature so that status updates are separated from the truly important information that its customers want their friends to see. This, it seems, is a reaction to a double twist with a high quality problem: there's now too much interesting stuff for everyone to digest all in one place.

Finally, it is impossible to ignore recent developments in a relatively long-winded competitive battle being played out between Apple and Samsung in the mobile phone and tablet markets.

Apple is alleging that Samsung, formerly an important partner, has copied the design features of its iPhone and iPad tablet devices and is using them to prop up their own sales. Samsung, on the other hand, is alleging that Apple has infringed its patents in both devices.

Both companies are demanding of the courts that their competitor's devices be blocked from sale.

There is only one reason this activity makes sense and it is this: both Samsung and Apple remain in a race to recruit users, because neither platform has decisively dominated. It is impossible to determine which will win: but, as we know from the sidestep and twist, it is the company with the most customers that usually does.

James Gardner
October, 2011

ABOUT THE AUTHOR

Dr. James Gardner is the chief technology officer of the UK's largest government department, Work and Pensions. Previously, he was head of innovation and research at Lloyds Banking Group. He is the author of *Innovation and the Future-proof Bank* (Wiley, 2009) and speaks and lectures around the world.